M000046110

THE
FOOTBALL
POCKET BIBLE

GAVIN COOKE

ACKNOWLEDGEMENTS

I would like to thank the following people for their assistance with this book: Holly Ivins for her infinite patience and guidance; Andrew Smith for his suggestions; Scott Reid and Andrew MacLaren for their inspirational trivia; and Paul McCormack and Josef Svernikov for keeping me right. Thanks also to Hugh Brune and Oliver Lester.

This edition first published in Great Britain 2010 by
Crimson Publishing, a division of Crimson Business Ltd
Westminster House
Kew Road
Richmond
Surrey
TW9 2ND

A catalogue record for this book is available from the British Library.

ISBN 978 1 907087 103

Printed and bound by Lego Print SpA, Trento

CONTENTS

FROM THE FIRST WHISTLE: THE HISTORY OF FOOTBALL

The history of football is a captivating and complex story. It has been filled with beauty, controversy and tragedy; moments of great joy and great sadness; life changing euphoria and heart-breaking disappointment. And then with every new season, a new page is turned and a new story is written.

🥾 FOOTBALL'S ANCESTORS 🥾

Activities involving the basic premise of football – two teams attempting to move a ball into their opponent's goal – have existed in different forms for centuries. In fact, more than two millennia ago, the ancient Chinese were playing a game, known as Tsu Chu, which involved kicking a ball into what could be referred to as a goal. However, it's more likely that the sport of association football that dominates the world today stems from the mass games played in Europe, and particularly Britain, during the Middle Ages.

These games, often referred to as mob football, involved two teams of unlimited size, with ill-defined rules attempting to move some form of ball to a recognised point. Violence was acceptable, although murder was frowned upon, and as there were no recognised 'pitches', property was often damaged as the game raged across fields and through streets. Although far removed from the modern professional game, the similarities to lower league football are clearly astounding.

Pocket Fact 🏆

There are references to football in two of Shakespeare's plays. In King Lear, Kent insults Oswald by referring to him as a 'base football player'. And in The Comedy of Errors, Dromio of Ephesus asks Adriana, the wife of his master: 'Am I so round with you, as you with me, that like a football you do spurn me thus? You spurn me hence, and he will spurn me hither: if I last in this service, you must case me in leather.'

👟 THE EARLY 1800s: 👟 REGULATIONS, RULES AND PUBLIC SCHOOLS

The rules surrounding mob football varied throughout countries, counties and even villages, and the game may have remained an occasional pastime were it not for the adoption of football by English public schools. By embracing the game, public schools paved the way for a more regulated version of the mob game. The number of players on each side was limited and the size of the pitch was restricted, signalling the foundation of modern football as we now recognise it.

Although the basics had been established, there were still fundamental variations between schools: for example, some schools allowed the ball to be carried and some required that it only be kicked. There was also vast disagreement on the level of violence which could be inflicted on the person with the ball. By the turn of the 19th century, these differences were becoming more pronounced.

Pocket Fact 🏆

English public schools (particularly Rugby School) were also responsible for the creation of rugby. Both rugby and association football share common roots and only began to move down different paths in the mid 1800s, when the schools that favoured rugby emphasised the importance of running with the ball in hand.

Boys moving on from public school to university took their enjoyment of their school's variation of football with them. However, this led to an obvious problem: the university students were unable to play the sport together as they all played using different rules. Fortunately, there was an obvious solution to this problem: the creation of a unified version of football rules using the best and most popular elements from each variant.

Written rules

- **1848**: Students at Cambridge University formulate the first written rules of football. These rules prevented players from handling the ball and hacking opponents.

- **1858**: The Sheffield rules are devised. These include the introduction of freekicks and throw-ins; but there was no rule concerning offside.

- **1863**: The London meetings which create the Football Association also produce a set of written rules, including an early version of the offside rule.

- **1877**: The FA rules and the Sheffield rules are unified – the FA accepts the introduction of throw-ins and Sheffield accepts the offside rule.

1860–1939: BIRTH OF ASSOCIATIONS, LEAGUES AND CUPS

THE FOOTBALL ASSOCIATION AND THE FA CUP

On 26 October 1863, the Football Association (FA), football's oldest governing body, was formed at a meeting held at the Freemason's Tavern in London. Initially, interest in the new organisation was limited and so in 1871 it was decided that a cup competition would be organised to encourage interest in the sport and its new ruling authority. Fifteen clubs entered the competition, which became known as the FA Cup, and the trophy was won by Wanderers, who defeated the Royal Engineers 1–0 in the final.

Pocket Fact 🏆

Queen's Park from Glasgow participated in the inaugural FA Cup, reaching the semi final without playing a game due to other teams withdrawing. However, they also withdrew after drawing their semi final match 0–0.

PROFESSIONALISM

As football's popularity grew, the northern clubs, dominated by the working classes, pushed for the legalisation of professionalism. However, the southern clubs, who wanted football to remain an amateur sport, strongly opposed this plan. By 1885 the northern clubs had won the argument and the FA accepted professionalism. Eight years later in 1893, the Scottish FA followed suit.

Key moments in the 19th century

- **1869**: Goal kicks introduced
- **1872**: Corner kicks introduced
- **1873**: Scottish FA formed in Glasgow
- **1874**: First shin pads appear
- **1876**: Welsh FA formed in Wrexham
- **1878**: Referees start using whistles
- **1880**: Irish FA formed in Belfast
- **1891**: Penalty kicks introduced in Football League – John Heath scores the first for Wolverhampton Wanderers

International matches

- The first ever international match was played between Scotland and England on 30 November 1872, and finished 0–0 (a scoreline not repeated until 1970).

- England recorded the first international victory, beating Scotland 4–2 at the Oval in 1873.

- The first international tournament was the Home International Championship involving England, Scotland, Wales and Ireland. It began in 1884 with Scotland winning the inaugural competition.

Half Time Quiz ⚽

Who is the only player to have scored a goal for two different nations at the World Cup finals?

(Answer: Robert Prosinečki. He scored for Yugoslavia at the 1990 World Cup and Croatia at the 1998 World Cup.)

THE FOOTBALL LEAGUE

The success of the FA Cup led to a desire for more competitive fixtures, and the inevitable result of this was the creation of a national league.

The Football League was created at a meeting held in Manchester on 17 April 1888. The 12 founding clubs who played in the first ever league season in 1888–1889 were Accrington, Aston Villa, Blackburn Rovers, Bolton, Burnley, Derby County, Everton, Notts County, Preston North End, Stoke, West Bromwich Albion, and Wolverhampton Wanderers. The popularity of the league led to the creation of the Second Division in 1892. Preston won the debut League (without losing a game) and the FA Cup (without conceding a goal), making them undefeated in all 27 of their competitive games that season.

The Scottish League soon followed in the 1890–1891 season. The 11 founding Scottish Clubs were Abercorn, Celtic, Cowlairs,

Cambuslang, Dumbarton, Hearts, Rangers, St Mirren, Renton, Third Lanark and Vale of Leven.

FIFA

FIFA (Fédération Internationale de Football Association) is football's global governing body. Its main roles include organising the World Cup competitions, contributing to the maintenance of the rules of the game, and ensuring that national football associations remain free from government interference.

- **1904**: FIFA formed at a meeting in Paris by representatives of the national associations of France, Belgium, Denmark, Netherlands, Spain, Sweden and Switzerland. The British associations had been asked to attend but declined the invitation. They did join the following year.

- **1909**: FIFA becomes global when South Africa joins. Argentina and Chile followed in 1912 and the United States in 1913.

- **1930**: The first World Cup takes place in Uruguay.

- **1974**: João Havelange becomes FIFA president and pushes through a series of reforms, turning FIFA into a modern institution.

- **2007**: Montenegro becomes the 208th affiliated member of FIFA (the United Nations can only boast 192 member states).

THE FIRST WORLD CUP

FIFA had been eager to organise its own international football tournament since its inception. Football had been very popular at the Olympic Games since its introduction in 1900 and this had only increased the desire of FIFA's French president, Jules Rimet, to establish a new independent competition. And so at the 1928 FIFA Congress, the delegates voted to create the World Cup. The inaugural tournament took place in 1930 in Uruguay and the hosts were rewarded with a 4–2 victory in the final over Argentina. Football's crown jewel had been born.

Half Time Quiz ☻

The Home Nations initially refused to participate in the World Cup due to a dispute with FIFA over professionalism. Which was the first World Cup tournament that a Home Nation took part in?

(Answer: England took part in the 1950 World Cup held in Brazil.)

👟 FOOTBALL DURING THE FIRST 👟 AND SECOND WORLD WARS

In England, the First World War led to the League, the FA Cup, and all international matches being suspended after the end of the 1914–1915 season. Football became restricted to regional leagues and players were no longer allowed to be paid. In 1939, the Football League was stopped almost immediately after the Second World War began. However, throughout Britain regional leagues were set up, although crowds were limited and teams were allowed to field guests to replace players who had joined the armed forces. Football also played an important part in maintaining morale; most army regiments had their own teams, and in some prisoner-of-war camps soldiers were able to organise leagues.

Early records

- Arbroath defeated Bon Accord 36–0 in the first round of the Scottish Cup in 1885. This remains the highest scoring match in the professional game.

- Liverpool were relegated from the First Division in the 1903–1904 season, even though they scored one more goal than the League winners, Sheffield Wednesday.

- Huddersfield Town became the first team to win the First Division three years in a row between 1923 and 1926. Arsenal, Liverpool and Manchester United have all since equalled this record.

- Dixie Dean remains the record scorer in England's top division, managing 60 goals for Everton in the 1927–1928 season.

- Aston Villa still hold the record for most goals scored in England's top division: they managed 128 goals during the 1930–1931 season.

👟 1945–1969: FOOTBALL ON 👟 TELEVISION AND IN EUROPE

UEFA AND THE BEGINNING OF EUROPEAN CLUB COMPETITION

The years following the Second World War saw Europe become increasingly divided; however, football acted as a common language that brought the continent's clubs and nations together.

- **1954**: The Union of European Football Associations (UEFA) is set up at a meeting in Basel.

- **1955**: UEFA launches the European Cup (now known as the Champions League): a tournament for the champions of each member nation's football league. The Inter-Cities Fairs Cup also begins, and although initially not organised by UEFA, it later evolves into the UEFA Cup.

- **1960**: The first UEFA European Nations Cup (now known as the UEFA European Championship) is held in France. The Soviet Union become the first winners, defeating Yugoslavia 2–1 in the final.

- **1960**: The European Cup Winners' Cup is introduced for the winners of each nation's domestic cup competition.

Pocket Fact 🏆

Greece withdrew from the 1964 European Nations Cup after being drawn against Albania; the two nations were at war with each other.

FOOTBALL ON TELEVISION

Football has changed from a sport viewed only from the terraces, to a sport viewed mostly from armchairs. However, this shift has taken many years to develop.

Television milestones

- The BBC arranged a special friendly match between Arsenal and their reserve team to be shown on television in September 1937.

- An England versus Scotland match becomes the first international to be shown on television in 1938. Later the same year, the FA Cup final is also televised.

- ITV negotiated the rights to show a number of English First Division games in the 1960–1961 season. However, many teams were unwilling to allow their matches to be screened as they believed it would lead to a vast fall in attendances, and so the deal was scrapped.

- In 1964 the BBC introduced Match of the Day: a highlights programme. From 1966 it became available nationwide and has continued to be broadcast to this day.

- The 1970 World Cup was the first to be shown live and in colour on British television.

- Live League football returned in 1983 on both ITV and the BBC. As the decade advanced, both interest in televised football and the money involved increased exponentially.

Pocket Fact 🏆

UEFA prevents League football being broadcast live on television between the hours of 2.45pm and 5.15pm on Saturdays in both England and Scotland, to prevent falls in attendance at lower league games. This has led to many televised games being played on Sundays.

🥾 1970–1989: THE UGLY SIDE 🥾
OF THE BEAUTIFUL GAME

The 1970s and 1980s produced some of the greatest football the world had ever seen; however, the beauty produced on the field was sadly overshadowed by football's greatest problem: hooliganism. This was not a new problem; instances of hooligans causing trouble at matches stretch back to the 19th century, but the problem became widespread in Europe, and particularly Britain, in the 1970s.

- **1972**: After their victory in the European Cup Winners' Cup final in Barcelona, Rangers fans invade the pitch and clash with Spanish police, leading to the death of a supporter. Rangers are subsequently banned from European competition for two years.

- **1975**: Leeds are banned from European competition for four years when their fans riot after losing the European Cup final to Bayern Munich in Paris.

- **1985**: The FA Cup quarter final between Luton and Millwall, broadcast live on television, has to be temporarily stopped due to rioting Millwall fans.

- **1985**: Thirty-nine fans die at the European Cup final held at the Heysel stadium in Belgium, after they had attempted to escape charging Liverpool fans. As a result of this tragedy, UEFA banned English clubs from European competition indefinitely.

- **1988**: At the European Championships held in West Germany, nearly 400 England fans are arrested after England lose all three of their group games.

Pocket Fact 🏆

After the tragic events at the Heysel stadium in 1985, English clubs were banned from competing in Europe until the 1990–1991 season. Liverpool's ban lasted an extra year.

🥾 1990–PRESENT: NEW LEAGUES, 🥾 NEW LAWS, MORE MONEY

TWO NEW LEAGUES

From humble beginnings in a London pub in 1863, football has grown to become the world's most popular sport: a fact underlined by the success of two new competitions created in the early 1990s.

- Towards the end of the 1980s, the revenues generated by television income began to increase at an exponential rate. Clubs in the English First Division wanted a greater share of this money and eventually decided that the best way to achieve this would be to break away from the Football League and form a new organisation.

- The FA Premier League came into being at the beginning of the 1992–1993 season. Initially the League consisted of 22 teams, but this was reduced to 20 at the start of the 1995–1996 season.

- Manchester United won the Premier League in its debut season; they remain one of only four teams to have won the Premier League title. The others are Arsenal, Chelsea and Blackburn Rovers.

- UEFA were also keen to take advantage of the growth in television revenues, and in the 1992–1993 season the Champions League replaced the European Cup. Instead of a straight knock-out tournament, the format was changed to include a qualifying round followed by a group stage. Further changes were made in the 1997–1998 season to give teams from the top-ranked nations who had not won their national league a place in the competition.

- Currently a maximum of four teams from a single nation can qualify for the Champions League.

Pocket Fact 🏆

The 2009 Champions League final was the world's most watched sporting event; it surpassed viewing figures for the American NFL's Super Bowl for the first time.

THE BOSMAN RULING

In December 1995 the Belgian player, Jean-Marc Bosman, won a ruling from the European Court of Justice which would fundamentally alter the nature of football in Europe. The ruling affected football in two major ways:

- It allowed players to leave clubs once their contracts had expired. Previously, teams in most European nations could prevent a player from leaving unless they were paid a transfer fee. This has resulted in an increase in the power that individual players hold.

- In European competitions, the 'three foreigner rule' had applied. This had meant that clubs competing in the three major European club competitions could only field three players that were not nationals of the association that the club played in. For example, Manchester United could only field three non-English players, AC Milan only three non-Italians, or Barcelona only three non-Spaniards. The court ruling decreed that this amounted to a restriction of trade and was therefore illegal in the European Union, and so this rule was abolished. The change in law has allowed clubs to field teams that do not include any home-grown players in their starting line-ups – a situation that occurred in the 2010 Champions League final when Internazionale's starting 11 included four Argentinians, three Brazilians, one Romanian, one Dutchman, and one Macedonian – but no Italians.

2

THAT'S NEVER A FOUL! THE RULES OF THE GAME

*The trouble with referees is that they know the rules,
but they do not know the game.*
Bill Shankly

👟 THE 17 RULES OF FOOTBALL 👟

The laws of the game are the same throughout the world; the rules used by the referee in the World Cup final are the same as the rules used by a referee in a local Sunday league match. Although a large proportion of the controversy surrounding football comes from disagreements over refereeing decisions, the rules themselves are surprisingly straightforward. There are 17 official rules laid down by FIFA and the IFAB (International Football Association Board) and they each deal with a different element of the game, covering both physical aspects and the way in which the players behave.

INTERNATIONAL FOOTBALL ASSOCIATION BOARD (IFAB)

The International Football Association Board (IFAB) was formed in 1882 by the football associations of England, Wales, Ireland and Scotland, to maintain a common set of rules for football. Each association had two votes and changes to the laws of the game could only be made by a three-quarters majority.

In 1913, FIFA was granted membership to the IFAB and given four votes, while the British associations' votes were reduced to one each. This situation continues to the present day and all changes to the laws of football, such as alterations to the offside rule, are decided by the IFAB.

RULE 1: THE SIZE OF THE PITCH

The measurements of each pitch must be as follows:

- **Length**: between 90m and 120m (100 yards and 130 yards)
- **Width**: between 45m and 90m (50 yards and 100 yards)

Pocket Fact 🏆

The two lines running the length of the pitch are called the touch lines, and the two lines running the width of the pitch are called the goal lines.

RULE 2: THE BALL

The ball must be spherical and made of either leather or a suitable synthetic material. The measurements of the ball must be as follows:

- **Circumference**: between 68cm and 70cm (27 inches and 28 inches)
- **Weight**: between 410g and 450g (14oz and 16oz)

If the ball bursts during play, the game is stopped and the referee restarts the match by dropping the new ball at the place where the original ball became defective.

Pocket Fact 🏆

The oldest surviving football dates from the 1540s and is made from a pig's bladder. It was found in Stirling Castle in 1981.

RULE 3: THE NUMBER OF PLAYERS

Each team is made up of 11 players, one of whom must be a goalkeeper. Both teams must have at least seven players at all times in the match. A maximum of three substitutes can be used during the course of a game.

Pocket Fact 🏆

A 2002 league match between Sheffield United and West Bromwich Albion was abandoned after Sheffield United were reduced to six men through a combination of red cards and injuries. WBA were winning 3–0 and the result was allowed to stand.

RULE 4: EQUIPMENT

Each player must wear a shirt with sleeves, shorts, shin guards, socks and footwear. The two teams must wear colours distinct from each other and from the referee. The two goalkeepers must wear a colour different from the other players and the referee.

Pocket Fact 🏆

At the 2002 African Cup of Nations, Cameroon fell foul of FIFA by wearing a sleeveless shirt and they had to have a new strip made for the World Cup held later in the same year.

RULE 5: THE REFEREE

The referee has full control over the match and their decision is final. The referee may reverse a decision as long as the match has not restarted or the final whistle has been blown.

Refereeing Disasters

Managers never tire of complaining about the standard of refereeing: it gives them someone else to blame when things go wrong. However, there have been a few rare occasions when the moaning managers do actually have a point. Here are a few examples of spectacular refereeing mistakes:

- *Croatia versus Australia 2006 World Cup group stage*: *English referee Graham Poll yellow carded Croatian defender Josip Simunic three times before sending him off. Poll, who had been one of the favourites to referee the World Cup final, was sent home early from the tournament.*
- *France versus Kuwait 1982 World Cup group stage*: *After France had scored a disputed goal, the head of the Kuwaiti FA, Sheikh Fahid Al-Ahmad Al-Sabah, rushed onto the pitch to protest the decision. The Russian referee, Miroslav Stupor, then decided to disallow the goal. Stupor never refereed an international match again.*
- *France versus West Germany 1982 World Cup semi final*: *Talented French defender Patrick Battiston was through on goal when German goalkeeper, Harald Schumacher, rushed off his line and ran straight into Battiston, knocking him unconscious, in one of the worst fouls ever seen at the World Cup. The referee, Charles Corver of the Netherlands, awarded a goal kick.*

RULE 6: THE REFEREE'S ASSISTANTS

Two assistant referees help the referee to control the game. Their main duties are adjudging when the ball has left the field of play or entered the goal; deciding which team should be awarded throw-ins, corner kicks, and goal kicks; and penalising players for being offside.

Pocket Fact 🏆

During the 2009–2010 Europa League, UEFA experimented with the introduction of two extra officials, who stood behind either goal line to help spot rule infringements in the penalty area.

RULE 7: LENGTH OF MATCHES

Each match lasts for a period of 90 minutes. Matches are divided into two periods of 45 minutes and between each period there is a 15 minute half time interval. Time is added on at the end of each half by the referee to allow for the time taken for substitutions, injuries to players, and for time wasting.

Pocket Fact 🏆

Referees add 30 seconds of additional time to the end of each half for every substitution made during the half.

RULE 8: KICK-OFF

A coin is tossed before the start of each match and the winning team decides which direction they wish to shoot. The team that lost the coin toss kicks off by hitting the ball forward from the centre spot: when this happens, all players must be in their own half. In the second half the teams change ends and the team that won the coin toss kicks off. The match is also restarted by a kick-off after a goal is scored. The team that conceded the goal kicks off.

Pocket Fact 🏆

A goal can be scored direct from the kick-off.

RULE 9: OUT OF PLAY

The ball is out of play when either the referee has stopped the game, or when the whole ball has crossed the touch line or the goal line. The ball remains in play if it rebounds off the frame of the goal or a corner flag.

Half Time Quiz ⚽

A player hits a shot that is heading wide of the goal, but the ball strikes the referee and goes into the goal. What should the referee award?

(Answer: The referee would award a goal because the ball is technically 'in play'.)

RULE 10: SCORING GOALS

A goal is scored when the whole ball crosses the goal line between the two goal posts and under the crossbar.

Did it Cross the Line?

Deciding whether the ball has crossed the goal line when the penalty box is crowded with players and the ball is moving quickly can be extremely difficult, and on some occasions referees get it wrong. Here are some of the most famous examples of referees making the wrong call:

- During a 2005 English Premiership match between Manchester United and Tottenham, Tottenham player Pedro Mendes hit a shot from the halfway line and Manchester United goalkeeper, Roy Carroll, fumbled the ball. It clearly crossed the line, but neither the assistant referee nor the referee awarded a goal.

- During the 1997 FA Cup semi final between Chesterfield Town and Middlesbrough, Chesterfield player Jonathon Howard hit a shot that struck the crossbar, then bounced behind the goal line while his side were leading 2–1. The referee failed to award a goal and Middlesbrough went on to draw the match 3–3 and win the replay.

- Without doubt, the most famous disputed goal of all time occurred during the 1966 World Cup final between West Germany and England. Geoff Hurst hit a shot during extra time that struck the crossbar and then bounced downwards. The Russian linesman, Tofik Bakhramov, awarded a goal. The debate over whether the ball actually crossed the line continues to this day.

- Frank Lampard's disallowed goal against Germany in the 2010 World Cup has now rivalled this disputed goal.

RULE 11: OFFSIDE

A player is offside when all of the following conditions are fulfilled:

- They are in the opponent's half.

- There are less than two opposition players closer to, or an equal distance from, the opponent's goal line.

- The ball is in the opposition half.

- The ball has been played forward.

- The player is interfering with play, meaning they have touched the ball or gained an advantage from being in that position.

If a player is caught offside, the referee awards an indirect free kick (see Rule 12 for an explanation of the types of free kick) to the opposing team.

Pocket Fact 🏆

A player cannot be offside if he receives the ball direct from a goal kick, a corner kick, or a throw-in.

RULE 12: PUNISHMENTS FOR MISCONDUCT

Direct free kicks

These are awarded for fouls and deliberate infringements. The player taking a direct free kick is allowed to score. Direct free kicks are awarded if a player:

- Trips or attempts to trip an opponent

- Kicks or attempts to kick an opponent

- Jumps at an opponent

- Charges an opponent

- Strikes an opponent

- Pushes an opponent

- Holds an opponent

- Spits at an opponent

- Handles the ball deliberately (excepting goalkeepers)

- Uses excessive force while tackling an opponent

Indirect free kicks

These are awarded for technical infringements and obstructing play. A player taking an indirect free kick is not allowed to score; the ball must touch at least one other player after an indirect free kick is taken before a goal can be scored. Indirect free kicks are awarded to the opposing team if a player:

- Behaves in a dangerous manner

- Obstructs an opponent

- Prevents the goalkeeper from releasing the ball

- Is caught offside

Indirect free kicks are also awarded to the opposing team if the goalkeeper:

- Holds the ball in his hands for more than six seconds

- Picks up the ball after releasing it from his hands without it touching another player

- Picks up the ball after it has been deliberately kicked to him by a member of his own team

- Picks up the ball direct from a throw-in, taken by a member of his own team

Yellow Cards (Cautions)

Also known as being 'booked', yellow cards are shown to players for:

- Unsporting behaviour (this includes celebrating a goal in an over-exuberant manner, feigning injury and fouling)

- Dissent (this includes consistently challenging the referee's decisions)

- Persistently breaking the rules of the game

- Delaying the restart of play

- Not retreating the required distance at a free kick, corner or throw-in

- Entering the field of play without the permission of the referee
- Leaving the field of play without the permission of the referee

Pocket Fact 🏆

All 11 players in a team can be booked, as can any unused substitute.

Red Cards (Sending Off)

These are shown to players for:

- Serious foul play
- Violent conduct
- Spitting at any person
- Denying the opposing team a clear goal scoring opportunity
- Using offensive language or gestures
- Receiving two yellow cards

If a player is given a red card they must immediately leave the pitch. If more than four players are sent off from either team, the match is abandoned.

Players who are red-carded are also automatically given a one match suspension (this means they are forced to miss the next league or cup game). This suspension can be increased if the football authorities feel that the offence is worthy of greater punishment.

Pocket Fact 🏆

Claudio Cannigia was named in the Argentina squad for the 2002 World Cup but did not play a match. However, he did manage to be sent off; during a group match against Sweden, Cannigia was sent off for dissent after he directed a tirade of abuse at the referee from his seat on the substitutes' bench. Cannigia had also missed the 1990 World Cup final due to suspension after being yellow-carded in the semi final.

RULE 13: FREE KICKS

There are two different types of free kicks: direct and indirect (see Rule 12 for an explanation of the differences between the two). Players can score goals straight from direct free kicks, but cannot do so from indirect free kicks.

For both types of free kick:

- The opposing team must be at least 9.15m (10 yards) from the ball.

- The player who takes the free kick cannot touch the ball again until it has touched another player.

- The ball must be stationary when the free kick is taken.

Half Time Quiz ⚽

A team has a direct free kick just outside their own penalty area. The player taking it attempts to pass back to the goalkeeper but the ball goes into the goal without any player touching it. What should the referee award?

(Answer: The referee would award a corner to the opposing team, as an own goal cannot be scored directly from a direct free kick.)

RULE 14: PENALTY KICKS

If a foul that would normally result in a direct free kick is committed inside the penalty area, a penalty is awarded. For a penalty kick to be legal, the ball must be placed on the penalty spot; the player taking the penalty must be clearly identified and must kick the ball forward; the goalkeeper must remain on the goal line until the ball has been kicked; and the other players must be outside the penalty area and at least 9.15m from the penalty spot.

Half Time Quiz ⚽

Prior to a penalty being taken, a player on the opposition team enters the penalty area. The penalty is taken and the goalkeeper makes a save. What should the referee do?

(Answer: The referee orders that the penalty be retaken. If the penalty had been scored, the goal would be allowed to stand.)

RULE 15: THROW-INS

If a player is the last to touch the ball before it leaves the field of play by crossing one of the touchlines, the opposing team are awarded a throw-in. For a throw-in to be legal, the player taking it must: face the field, take the throw-in from the place where the ball left the field, have part of both feet outside the field of play and touching the ground, hold the ball with two hands, and deliver the ball into the field of play from behind their head.

Pocket Fact 🏆

Danny Brooks, an English PE teacher, holds the world record for the longest throw-in. He threw the ball almost 50 metres, which is equivalent to half the length of a football field.

RULE 16: GOAL KICKS

A goal kick is awarded if the attacking team hits the whole ball over the goal line. For a goal kick to be legal, it must be taken within the goal area and the players on the opposing team must be outside the penalty area. No player from either team is allowed to touch the ball after a goal kick until it has left the penalty area.

Half Time Quiz ⚽

A goalkeeper takes a goal kick, but due to freak high winds the ball is blown back over his head and into his own goal. What is the correct decision?

(Answer: The referee would award a corner to the opposing team as an own goal cannot be scored direct from a goal kick. However, if the freak winds had blown in the other direction and the ball had ended up in the opposition goal without touching another player, the goal would stand.)

RULE 17: CORNER KICKS

A corner kick is awarded if the defending team hits the whole ball over the goal line.

Corner kicks must be taken in the corner arc closest to where the ball left the field and must be taken by a player from the attacking team. Goals can be scored direct from corner kicks.

Pocket Fact 🏆

In South America, goals scored direct from corners are called 'Olympic Goals'. This is because in 1924 Argentina scored a goal of this type against Uruguay, who were the current Olympic champions.

👟 CHANGES TO THE LAWS 👟 OF THE GAME

The rules of football have not remained static throughout its 150 years of history. Changes in the rules, both major and minor, have allowed the game to move with the times and remain a thoroughly modern sport.

OFFSIDE

In football's infancy in the 19th century, any attacking player who was in front of the ball was deemed to be offside. Over time, this rule has evolved into the form that exists today:

- In the late 1860s, the FA decided that a player was only offside if there were fewer than three defenders between him and the goal.

- In 1925, in order to encourage a more attack-based game, a player was only offside if there were fewer than two defenders between him and the goal.

- In 1990 a further change was made; a player was now onside if he was level with the second last defender.

Pocket Fact 🏆

Filippo Inzaghi, the AC Milan forward, has been caught offside so often that Alex Ferguson once claimed: 'Filippo Inzaghi was born in an offside position.'

SUBSTITUTIONS

Substitutions were introduced because prior to this, injured players had to continue playing and this was ruining some matches. One substitute was allowed in the Football League in England in the 1965–1966 season; however, the substitute could only replace an injured player. At the start of the 1966–1967 season, the rule was changed to allow a substitute to be used for any reason. In 1988 the IFAB changed the law to allow two substitutes to be used. The law was further altered in 1994 to allow a third substitution to be made, but only to substitute the goalkeeper. The most recent change to the law occurred in 1995 and allowed the third substitute to replace any player. In the modern game, substitutions allow managers the opportunity to make tactical changes to their team, to replace underperforming players or to give inexperienced younger players the chance to gain experience.

3

SYSTEMS, SHAPE, STYLE AND SPACE: FOOTBALL TACTICS

Formations and tactics are the means by which a manager controls the way his team plays. Essentially, the formation deals with the shape of a team – how many defenders, midfielders and forwards there will be – and tactics deal with the style and mind-set that each player adopts. From this basic premise springs all of the vast complexity and obscure technical language that surrounds the issue of tactics in football. However, cutting through the jungle of jargon reveals one simple truth: formations and tactics are used by managers to maximise space for their own players and limit it for the opposition.

THE PHILOSOPHY OF TACTICS

Good managers have their own tactics and shape their players to fit it; great managers identify their players' strengths and build their tactics around these. But the greatest managers adopt a process of permanent evolution, changing their tactics constantly and leaving behind effective styles once they have worn out their usefulness.

CHANGING TACTICS

Over time, football tactics have become more conservative and the number of goals scored in each match has decreased. Spectators at the early World Cups enjoyed matches which averaged between four and five goals; however, by the 1990 World Cup, fans were lucky to see more than two goals during a game. This change can be explained by the fact that the early football teams of the late 19th century were hugely biased in favour of attack and it was common to have six or even eight forwards. However, as time has passed, the number of forwards has decreased and players have been given more defined roles to perform.

CHANGING POSITIONS

Radical change in football formations has led to the disappearance of some positions, including:

- **Inside Forward**. These played on either side of the centre forward in the early 20th century formations which included five attackers.

- **Outside Forward**. The two widest players in the front five formation mentioned above.

- **Half Back**. Early formations often included two players occupying the middle of the pitch. These players would support the inside forwards in an attacking capacity and the full backs in a defensive role.

👟 MODERN FORMATIONS 👟

Football tactics are rapidly becoming as complicated as the chemical formula for splitting the atom.
Jimmy Greaves

Formations are commonly expressed by a series of numbers: for example, 4-4-2, where the first number indicates the number of defenders, the second indicates the number of midfielders, and the third the number of forwards.

MODERN POSITIONS: WHO'S WHO ON THE PITCH

While it may seem that there are a huge number of positions in the modern game, the overwhelming majority of teams only use the following positions:

- **Centre backs**. The defenders who play in the centre of the defensive line. Their job is to mark the opposition centre forwards and clear the ball when it is crossed into the box.

Most teams play with two centre backs, but some teams play with three. Modern centre backs include John Terry and Lúcio.

- **Full backs**. The defenders who play on either wing. Their job is to mark the opposition wide players and to prevent the ball being crossed into the box. In the modern game, full backs are also expected to help out when their team is attacking. Full backs are usually among the fastest players in the team. Ashley Cole and Philipp Lahm are two of the modern game's best full backs.

- **Centre midfielders**. The midfielders who play in the middle of the pitch. They are usually the fittest players in the team, as they are expected to both defend and attack. They make tackles and mark opposition midfielders when the opposition has the ball, and help out their forwards when their own team has the ball. Most teams play with either two or three centre midfielders. The Spaniards Xavi and Cesc Fàbregas are among the world's best central midfielders.

- **Wide midfielders**. Wide midfielders play on either wing of the midfield. Their job is to cross the ball into the opposition box and to support their forwards. Wide midfielders are also required to track the runs of opposition full backs. Wide midfielders are usually the most skilful players in the team. Arjen Robben and Cristiano Ronaldo are two of the world's best wide players.

- **Centre forwards**. Centre forwards have the most straightforward role: they are simply required to score goals. There are many different types of centre forwards, from fast and skilful players, such as Jermaine Defoe, to tall and strong players, such as Didier Drogba.

Picking a formation is a difficult science, which requires a balance between exploiting the strengths of the players available and the weaknesses of opponents. However, the purpose of football is to entertain: this means that managers must also strike a balance between the supporters' desire to see their team win, and their desire to see their team play attractive football. Keeping all these plates spinning at once can often lead to a manager's downfall.

The most common modern formations, along with their advantages and disadvantages are detailed below.

FOUR-FOUR-TWO

The 4-4-2 formation is composed of:

- Four defenders
- Four midfielders
- Two forwards

This formation provides a good balance between attack and defence and because of this it is one of the most commonly used formations in the modern game. In this formation:

- The wide players (the full backs and the left and right midfielders) help each other out to provide extra numbers when the team is attacking or defending.

- One of the central midfielders usually pushes forward to help the forwards, while the other central midfielder sits back to protect the defence (this is often referred to as the 'holding role').

- The two forwards focus almost entirely on attack, and are often required to put the opposition defenders under pressure when the other team is in possession of the ball.

Pocket Fact 🏆
During the 1960s, Russian manager Victor Maslov altered the 4-2-4 formation by moving the two wingers back into midfield, thus pioneering the 4-4-2 formation.

One of the disadvantages of this formation is that the wide players must be effective both offensively and defensively, which can force a manager to choose the mediocre but consistent over those who are exceptionally talented in only one area.

Famous 4-4-2 teams:

- AC Milan's 1994 Champions League winning team

- Manchester United's 1999 Champions League winning team

- Arsenal's 2003–2004 undefeated Premier League winning team

Great tactical innovations: The 'WM' formation

In 1925 the offside rule was altered so that only two players had to be between the forward and the goal instead of three. The Arsenal manager, Herbert Chapman, took full advantage of the new rule to move away from the traditional 2-3-5 formation and created the WM formation (so called as the players lined up in the shape of a W and an M). The key innovation of this new style was withdrawing the centre half from midfield and placing them in defence to mark the opposition centre forward. Using 'WM', Chapman went on to twice win the English First Division with Arsenal, and soon many teams throughout England, and the world, were copying his new style.

FOUR-THREE-THREE

The 4-3-3 formation is composed of:

- Four defenders

- Three midfielders

- Three forwards

The 4-3-3 formation is a more attacking formation than 4-4-2, and it requires a large degree of positional discipline from the players. In this formation:

- The four defenders line up in the same way as in the 4-4-2 formation, but the full backs are expected to concentrate less on attacking.

- The three midfield players tend to play close together as a unit to prevent the opposition from overwhelming the defence.

- In contrast, the three forward players spread out across the pitch to provide width to the team's attacks, and to cause problems for the opposition defenders who are tasked with marking them.

Pocket Fact 🏆

During the 1966 World Cup, the England manager Alf Ramsey sometimes used a 4-3-3 formation, which became known in some quarters as 'the wingless wonders' because there were no wingers in the team and wonders.

The 4-3-3 formation is commonly used against weaker teams, but against more effective opposition it can lead to a team being over-run in the midfield area. However, teams with a wealth of attacking options often employ this formation as it allows them to exploit their strengths.

Famous 4-3-3 teams:

- Brazil's 1970 World Cup winning team

- Argentina's 1978 World Cup winning team

- Barcelona's 2009 Champions League winning team

Great tactical innovations: Catenaccio

Catenaccio (from the Italian for 'door bolt') is a defensive style of football whose key feature was the use of a sweeper. The sweeper was a defensive player who sat behind a line of four defenders; their job was to 'sweep up' any loose balls and to negate the threat of the opposition forwards. As playing with a sweeper means sacrificing either a forward or midfielder, games involving teams which employed the Catenaccio system were often low-scoring affairs. This system, which was most commonly associated with Italian teams, has dropped out of use in the modern game mainly due to the increasing fluidity of midfielders and forwards, and the decline in use of sweepers.

FOUR-FIVE-ONE

The 4-5-1 formation is composed of:

- Four defenders
- Five midfielders
- One forward

The 4-5-1 formation is often used by teams who are defending a lead (for example in the second leg of a cup tie), or playing against superior opposition. This formation relies on:

- The five players in midfield working hard to stifle the opposing team's forward players by preventing them from receiving passes, and closing them down quickly when they do gain possession.

- The solitary forward holding on to the ball when they gain possession, as they are often very isolated.

- The wide midfielders supporting the forward to provide extra numbers in attack.

This formation works most effectively when a team can field five midfielders with a high level of physical fitness, as this allows them to carry out their defensive duties and help the lone striker.

Famous 4-5-1 teams:

- Italy's 1982 World Cup winning team
- France's 1998 World Cup winning team
- Chelsea's 2004–2005 Premier League winning team

Pocket Fact 🏆

Rangers' style of play in their run to the 2008 UEFA Cup final became so synonymous with defensive football that Rangers fans dubbed it 'Watenaccio': a reference to both the Catenaccio style and Walter Smith, the Rangers manager.

🥾 ATTACKING TACTICS 🥾

*Simple football is the most beautiful. But playing simple
football is the hardest thing.*
Johan Cruyff

Formations control the way that players set themselves up on the
pitch, but tactics influence the style with which they play the
game. Attacking tactics are the methods that a manager wants his
team to use when they are in possession of the ball.

COUNTER-ATTACKING

Teams that employ the counter-attacking style can often be the
most entertaining to watch. Teams that use this style must:

- Retreat into their own half to encourage their opponent to
  commit a significant number of players forward.

- Leave one or two forwards in an advanced position.

- Launch a fast attack as soon as they regain possession of the
  ball, so that the opposing team does not have time to regain
  their defensive shape.

This style is often used by teams who are defending a lead: however, some teams use this style permanently, such as the United
States national team.

Great tactical innovations: Total Football

*Rinus Michels, as the manager of Ajax, Barcelona, and most
famously the Dutch national team, created a revolutionary
footballing philosophy whereby each outfield player could carry
out any role on the pitch. For example, a centre forward could
become a left-back, or a centre back could become a right
winger. This creates a team that is both quick to adapt and
ruthless in exploiting opposition weaknesses. The Dutch
national team was the most famous exponent of this system;
using it they reached the final of both the 1974 and 1978
World Cups, although they lost both matches.*

> *Teams employing Total Football must possess a large number of highly skilful and physically fit players; as few teams can boast these riches, this system is rarely seen in the modern game.*

DIRECT

This footballing philosophy is also referred to as 'long ball' or 'Route 1' football. For this style of play to be successful, teams must:

- Repeatedly play high passes to a forward (often referred to as the 'target man'), whose job it is to attempt a shot on goal or to keep possession until his teammates can join in the attack.

- Play with a target man who is both strong and tall in order to allow him to gain possession of the ball, and to prevent the opposition defenders from taking it from him. Famous target men include Jan Koller, Peter Crouch and Chris Sutton.

Direct football is most commonly used by lower league teams, mainly because it relies on physical attributes rather than the rarer commodity of technical ability, but some higher level clubs such as Bolton have been able to achieve a relatively high degree of success while utilising this form of the game.

Pocket Fact 🏆

The invention of the direct style is often credited to former accountant and RAF veteran Charles Reep. In the 1950s, Reep subjected football to a statistical analysis and concluded that the fewer passes a team completes before taking a shot, the more likely they are to score. This conclusion led him to agitate for the introduction of the long ball game.

POSSESSION

This style of play is difficult to perfect, but when used effectively it can produce beautiful football. The theory behind possession football is:

- A team retains possession for an extended period by completing a series of passes which forces the opposition to chase the ball.

- This tires opposition players out and can lead them to be dragged out of position, thus creating space which the attacking team can exploit.

Players involved in this system must be accurate passers, confident on the ball, and possess good footballing intelligence. Modern teams who employ the possession style of football include Barcelona and Arsenal.

Pocket Fact 🏆

One of the most impressive examples of the possession style came in a group match between Argentina and Serbia and Montenegro at the 2006 World Cup. The Argentinian team completed 24 passes before midfielder Esteban Cambiasso rounded off the move with a left foot drive past the Serbian goalkeeper.

👟 DEFENSIVE TACTICS 👟

The best place to defend is in the opposition penalty box.
Jock Stein

As mentioned above, defending has become an increasingly important aspect of football, and this has led to the development of many innovative and contrasting defensive tactics.

MAN-TO-MAN MARKING AND ZONAL DEFENCE

There are two basic defensive styles: man-to-man marking and zonal defence.

Teams using man-to-man marking:

- Allocate a defensive player to follow around (or 'mark') an opposing forward.

- Each defender must try to prevent the player they are marking from receiving the ball, and tackle them if they do manage to gain possession.

- Often at least one player is not allocated an opposition player: instead they are left 'spare'. Their job is to provide cover should an opposing forward manage to evade their marker.

Teams utilising zonal defence:

- Organise their midfield and defenders into two straight lines and allocate each player a 'zone' to defend.

- When the opposition players bring the ball forward, both lines of defenders move together as a unit, thus preventing any spaces appearing that the opposition can exploit.

- Unlike man-to-man marking, where a defender can follow the forward they are marking anywhere, defenders in the zonal system must never be dragged out of position.

In practice, most teams tend to use a mixture of both systems: for example, one defender will man-mark the most dangerous opposition forward while the others will adopt the zonal system.

Pocket Fact 🏆

Rafael Benitez's Liverpool team were famous for their use of the zonal defensive tactic when defending corners or free kicks into the penalty area. Their use of this system has inspired much debate in the media and amongst fans over its successfulness.

FORWARD OR RETREATING

As well as deciding what style of marking to use, managers must also decide where they want their defenders to start making tackles. In making this decision, managers must choose between the forward and retreating styles of play.

In the forward defensive style (often referred to as the 'pressing game'):

- A team attempts to win possession back as soon as they lose the ball, often making tackles and marking opposition players in the opposition half.

- If the defending team advances too far up the pitch, it can leave a space between the last line of defenders and the goal, which the opposing team can then exploit.

- This style of play requires a high level of physical fitness and can be difficult to maintain for a full match.

English club sides as well as the English national team have historically adopted this style of play.

Pocket Fact 🏆

The introduction of the 'pressing' style of football is viewed as one of the developments that have turned football into an increasingly physical and stamina-based game. In football's early years, it was common for players to enjoy a large amount of time on the ball before the opposition attempted to make a challenge.

The retreating defensive style involves:

- A team withdrawing back into their own half after losing the ball, only making tackles and marking opposition players once they have advanced beyond the halfway line.

- This style prevents space from developing behind the last defenders, but it does grant opposition players extra time on the ball and can lead to enough space being created to allow opposition forwards to take shots at goal from distance.

This style is most commonly associated with Italian and Iberian club sides and national teams.

Half Time Quiz ⚽

How many times have teams from the same country met in the European Cup/Champions League final?

(Answer: Three – 2008 (Manchester United versus Chelsea), 2003 (AC Milan versus Juventus), and 2000 (Real Madrid versus Valencia).)

THE OFFSIDE TRAP

The 'offside trap' is one of the oldest defensive tactics in football. Defenders using this tactic:

- Attempt to strand opposition forwards in an offside position by moving up the field just before the ball is played forward by the opposite team.

- For this style of play to be effective, the defenders must learn to move as a unit (and also shout, 'Offside, ref!' very loudly) in a straight line.

- One of the defenders, usually one of the centre backs, is given the responsibility of deciding when to move forward and the other defenders must mirror their movements.

This strategy can prove to be highly risky; if a forward manages to outwit the opposing defenders, they will usually have a clear run in on goal.

Pocket Fact 🏆

Former Arsenal manager George Graham became so adept at setting up his team to employ the offside trap that a favourite fans' chant became, 'One Nil to the Arsenal', in recognition of the scarcity of goals their team conceded.

4

PRIDE OF THE TOWN: FOOTBALL CLUBS

*In life a man can change wives, political parties, or religions,
but he cannot change his favourite football team.*
Eduardo Galleano

Football teams have become one of the most important parts of a town or city's identity. Here are the main teams in England and Scotland, as well as the most famous teams from around the world.

👟 ENGLISH PREMIER LEAGUE 👟

ARSENAL

Nickname: The Gunners
Ground: The Emirates Stadium, London
Honours: 13 League Championships; 10 FA Cups; two League Cups; one European Cup Winners' Cup; one Fairs Cup
Club Hero: Thierry Henry – fast and graceful striker who is Arsenal's all-time leading goal scorer and was a key member of the 'Invincibles' team, which won the Premier League title in the 2003–2004 season without losing a game.
Biggest Win: Arsenal 12 – Loughborough 0 (1900)
Biggest Defeat: Loughborough 8 – Arsenal 0 (1896)
Fan Fact: The three matches with the highest recorded attendances in the English top flight all involve Arsenal, but in all three Arsenal were the away team.
Best Pub for Away Fans: The Twelve Pins

ASTON VILLA

Nickname: The Villans
Ground: Villa Park, Birmingham
Honours: Seven League Championships; seven FA Cups; five League Cups; one European Cup; one European Super Cup
Club Hero: Peter Withe – forward who played for the club for five years and scored Villa's only goal in their famous 1982 European Cup triumph.
Biggest Win: Aston Villa 13 – Old Wednesbury Athletic 0 (1886)
Biggest Defeat: Blackburn Rovers 7 – Aston Villa 0 (1899)
Fan Fact: Aston Villa have provided more England internationals than any other club; 68 players have received at least one England cap while playing for Aston Villa.
Best Pub for Away Fans: The Barton Arms

BIRMINGHAM CITY

Nickname: The Blues
Ground: St Andrews Stadium, Birmingham
Honours: One League Cup
Club Hero: Trevor Francis – forward who remains the youngest Birmingham player to play in a league match, and is the club's leading league goal scorer in the post-war period.
Biggest Win: Birmingham 12 – Doncaster Rovers 0 (1903)
Biggest Defeat: Sheffield Wednesday 9 – Birmingham 1 (1930)
Fan Fact: Birmingham were the first English club to take part in a European club competition, participating in the Fairs Cup in 1956; they were also the first English club to reach a European final, reaching the Fairs Cup final in 1960.
Best Pub for Away Fans: The Anchor

BLACKBURN ROVERS

Nickname: The Rovers
Ground: Ewood Park, Blackburn
Honours: Three League Championships; six FA Cups; one League Cup
Club Hero: Jack Walker – chairman who turned Blackburn from a struggling Division One side into Premier League champions.

Biggest Win: Blackburn 11 – Rossendale United 0 (1884)
Biggest Defeat: Arsenal 8 – Blackburn 0 (1933)
Fan Fact: Blackburn are one of only two clubs who have won the FA Cup three years in succession: the triumphs came in 1884, 1885, and 1886.
Best Pub for Away Fans: The Fernhurst Arms

BLACKPOOL

Nickname: The Seasiders
Ground: Bloomfield Road, Blackpool
Honours: One FA Cup
Club Hero: Stanley Matthews – inspirational performance in the 1953 FA Cup final led to a Blackpool victory and the match going down in history as the 'Matthews Final'.
Biggest Win: Blackpool 10 – Lanerossi Vicenza (Italy) 0 (1972)
Biggest Defeat: Huddersfield Town 10 – Blackpool 1 (1930)
Fan Fact: The transfer of Alan Ball from Blackpool to Everton was the first six-figure transfer between two English clubs.
Best Pub for Away Fans: The Swift Hound

BOLTON WANDERERS

Nickname: The Trotters
Ground: Reebok Stadium, Bolton
Honours: Four FA Cups
Club Hero: Nat Lofthouse – centre forward who played for Bolton for his entire career from the 1940s to the 1960s, and scored both of Bolton's goals in their 1958 FA Cup win.
Biggest Win: Bolton 13 – Sheffield United 0 (1890)
Biggest Defeat: Preston 9 – Bolton 1 (1887)
Fan Fact: Bolton became the first team to score a goal at Wembley Stadium, when they defeated West Ham 2–0 in the 1923 FA Cup final.
Best Pub for Away Fans: The Bromilow Arms

CHELSEA

Nickname: The Blues
Ground: Stamford Bridge, London

Honours: Four League Championships; six FA Cups; four League Cups; two European Cup Winners' Cups; one European Super Cup

Club Hero: Roman Abramovich – billionaire Russian chairman who has bankrolled Chelsea's recent vast expenditure in the transfer market.

Biggest Win: Chelsea 13 – Jeunesse Hautcharage (Luxembourg) 0 (1971)

Biggest Defeat: Wolverhampton 8 – Chelsea 1 (1953)

Fan Fact: Former chairman Ken Bates bought Chelsea for £1 in 1982 as the club were mired in debt. Just over 20 years later, Abramovich paid £140 million to buy the club from Bates.

Best Pub for Away Fans: The Slug and Lettuce

EVERTON

Nickname: The Toffees

Ground: Goodison Park, Liverpool

Honours: Nine League Championships; five FA Cups; one European Cup Winners' Cup

Club Hero: Dixie Dean – forward who remains record scorer in England's top division, managing 60 goals in the 1927–1928 season.

Biggest Win: Everton 11 – Derby County 2 (1890)

Biggest Defeat: Sunderland 7 – Everton 0 (1934)

Fan Fact: In the 1933 FA Cup final, Everton became the first club to wear numbered shirts.

Best Pub for Away Fans: The Head of Steam

FULHAM

Nickname: The Cottagers

Ground: Craven Cottage, London

Honours: Two Tier Two titles; Two Tier Three titles

Club Hero: Johnny Haynes – inspirational forward who holds the record for most appearances for Fulham.

Biggest Win: Fulham 10 – Ipswich 1 (1963)

Biggest Defeat: Liverpool 10 – Fulham 0 (1986)

Fan Fact: Fulham's mascot, Billy the Badger, was sent off by the referee during a league game against Aston Villa in 2008 for delaying the start of the second half by dancing in the corner of the pitch.

Best Pub for Away Fans: The Eight Bells

LIVERPOOL

Nickname: The Reds
Ground: Anfield, Liverpool
Honours: 18 League Championships; seven FA Cups; seven League Cups; five European Cups; three UEFA Cups; three European Super Cups
Club Hero: Bill Shankly – manager who led Liverpool from the Second Division to three league titles, two FA Cups, and the club's first European trophy: the UEFA Cup.
Biggest Win: Liverpool 11 – Strømsgodset (Norway) 0 (1974)
Biggest Defeat: Birmingham 9 – Liverpool 1 (1954)
Fan Fact: In 1986, Liverpool became the first team in the history of the FA Cup final to field a starting 11 that did not include any English players. Liverpool won the match beating Everton 3–1.
Best Pub for Away Fans: The Arkles

Half Time Quiz ☻

Who are the only team to win the top division in England, and then be relegated in the next season?

(Answer: Manchester City. They won the top division in the 1936–1937 season, but finished 21st in the 1937–1938 season and were relegated even though they were the highest scorers in the league.)

MANCHESTER CITY

Nickname: City
Ground: The City of Manchester Stadium, Manchester
Honours: Two League Championships; four FA Cups; two League Cups; one European Cup Winners' Cup
Club Hero: Colin Bell – midfielder who played a central role in City's success in the late 1960s and early 1970s.
Biggest Win: Manchester City 12 – Liverpool Stanley 0 (1890)
Biggest Defeat: Everton 9 – Manchester City 1 (1906)
Fan Fact: Goalkeeper Bert Trautmann famously carried on playing in the 1956 FA Cup final (which City won 3–1) after he broke

his neck. As well as his FA Cup Winners' medal, Trautmann, a German, also won the Iron Cross while fighting on the Eastern Front during the Second World War.

Best Pub for Away Fans: The Crown and Cushion

MANCHESTER UNITED

Nickname: The Red Devils

Ground: Old Trafford, Manchester

Honours: 18 League Championships; 11 FA Cups; four League Cups; three European Cups; one European Cup Winners' Cup; one UEFA Super Cup; one FIFA Club World Cup

Club Hero: George Best – winger who was the club's top scorer for six successive seasons, and remains one of the greatest British footballers.

Biggest Win: Manchester United 10 – Anderlecht (Belgium) 0 (1956)

Biggest Defeat: Blackburn Rovers 7 – Manchester United 0 (1926)

Fan Fact: Tommy Docherty, the Manchester United manager between 1972 and 1977, was sacked not because of poor results, but because he had an affair with the wife of the team's physiotherapist.

Best Pub for Away Fans: Tollgate Inn

NEWCASTLE UNITED

Nickname: The Toon

Ground: St James' Park, Newcastle

Honours: Four League Championships; six FA Cups; one Fairs Cup

Club Hero: Jackie Milburn – Newcastle's second highest goal scorer; helped Newcastle to win three FA Cups in the 1950s and has a stand at St James' Park named after him.

Biggest Win: Newcastle 13 – Newport County 0 (1946)

Biggest Defeat: Burton Wanderers 9 – Newcastle 0 (1895)

Fan Fact: In the 19th century, Newcastle played in red and white stripes: now the colours of their fiercest rivals Sunderland.

Best Pub for Away Fans: The Centurion

STOKE CITY

Nickname: The Potters
Ground: Britannia Stadium, Stoke
Honours: One League Cup
Club Hero: Stanley Matthews – one of England's greatest ever players, played for Stoke until his 50th birthday, thus becoming the oldest player to play in England's top league.
Biggest Win: Stoke City 11 – Stourbridge 0 (1914)
Biggest Defeat: Preston North End 10 – Stoke City 0 (1889)
Fan Fact: During the break between the 1966–1967 and 1967–1968 seasons, Stoke City played in the United Soccer Association league in the USA as the Cleveland Stokers.
Best Pub for Away Fans: Trentham Lakes

SUNDERLAND

Nickname: The Black Cats
Ground: The Stadium of Light, Sunderland
Honours: Six League Championships; two FA Cups
Club Hero: Bob Stokoe – hat-wearing manager who took Sunderland to FA Cup glory in 1973, despite the fact that the club were outside of England's top division.
Biggest Win: Sunderland 11 – Fairfield 1 (1895)
Biggest Defeat: West Ham United 8 – Sunderland 0 (1968)
Fan Fact: In 1990, Sunderland lost the play-off final against Swindon Town to decide who would gain promotion to the top tier of the Football League. However, Swindon were found guilty of financial irregularities and Sunderland were promoted in their place.
Best Pub for Away Fans: The Albion

TOTTENHAM HOTSPUR

Nickname: Spurs
Ground: White Hart Lane, London
Honours: Two League Championships; eight FA Cups; four League Cups; two UEFA Cups; one European Cup Winners' Cup
Club Hero: Danny Blanchflower – skilful midfielder who formed the heart of the famous Spurs side of the early 1960s.

Biggest Win: Tottenham 13 – Crewe 2 (1960)
Biggest Defeat: FC Köln (Germany) 8 – Tottenham 0 (1995)
Fan Fact: In the 1960–1961 season, Tottenham became the first team in the 20th century to achieve the double of the league championship and FA Cup.
Best Pub for Away Fans: The Gilpin's Bell

WEST BROMWICH ALBION

Nickname: The Baggies
Ground: The Hawthorns, West Bromwich
Honours: One League Championship; five FA Cups; one League Cup
Club Hero: Jeff Astle – forward who scored in every round of the 1967–1968 FA Cup, including the only goal in Albion's victory over Everton in the final.
Biggest Win: West Brom 12 – Darwen 0 (1892)
Biggest Defeat: Stoke City 10 – West Brom 3 (1937)
Fan Fact: At 551 feet above sea level, the Hawthorns is the highest ground in the United Kingdom.
Best Pub for Away Fans: The Royal Oak

WEST HAM UNITED

Nickname: The Hammers
Ground: The Boleyn Ground (also known as Upton Park), London
Honours: Three FA Cups; one European Cup Winners' Cup
Club Hero: Bobby Moore – captained West Ham for over a decade and also captained England at their 1966 World Cup triumph.
Biggest Win: West Ham 10 – Bury 0 (1983)
Biggest Defeat: Everton 7 – West Ham 0 (1927)
Fan Fact: All four of England's goals in the 1966 World Cup final were scored by West Ham players: Geoff Hurst scored a hat-trick and Martin Peters scored the other goal.
Best Pub for Away Fans: The Millers Well

WIGAN ATHLETIC

Nickname: The Lactics
Ground: The DW Stadium, Wigan
Honours: One Tier Three title; one Tier Four title
Club Hero: Dave Whelan – chairman who took Wigan from the bottom of the lowest tier of the Football League to the Premier League.
Biggest Win: Wigan 7 – Scarborough 1 (1997)
Biggest Defeat: Tottenham 9 – Wigan 1 (2009)
Fan Fact: After repeatedly failing in their attempts to gain election to the Football League, Wigan applied to join the Scottish League in 1972. Somewhat unsurprisingly, their application was rejected. The club eventually gained League status in 1978.
Best Pub for Away Fans: The Red Robin

WOLVERHAMPTON WANDERERS

Nickname: Wolves
Ground: Molineux Stadium, Wolverhampton
Honours: Three League Championships; four FA Cups; two League Cups
Club Hero: Stan Cullis – influential defender, then manager of the club during its most successful period.
Biggest Win: Wolverhampton 14 – Cresswell's Brewery 0 (1886)
Biggest Defeat: Newton Heath 10 – Wolverhampton 1 (1892)
Fan Fact: In 1972 Tottenham and Wolverhampton Wanderers both reached the final of the European Cup Winners' Cup. It was the first all-British final of a European trophy. Tottenham triumphed 3–2 over two legs.
Best Pub for Away Fans: The Wheatsheaf Inn

🥾 ENGLISH CHAMPIONSHIP 🥾

BARNSLEY

Nickname: The Tykes
Ground: Oakwell, Barnsley

Honours: One FA Cup
Club Hero: Arthur Fairclough – manager who led Barnsley to their only major trophy success: the FA Cup in 1912.
Biggest Win: Barnsley 9 – Loughborough Town 0 (1899)
Biggest Defeat: Notts County 9 – Barnsley 0 (1927)
Fan Fact: Barnsley hold the record for most seasons spent in the second tier of English football.
Best Pub for Away Fans: The Outpost

BRISTOL CITY

Nickname: The Robins
Ground: Ashton Gate, Bristol
Honours: One Tier Two title
Club Hero: Trevor Tainton – midfielder who played a key role in helping City gain promotion to the top flight in the 1975–1976 season.
Biggest Win: Bristol City 11 – Chichester City 0 (1960)
Biggest Defeat: Coventry City 9 – Bristol City 0 (1934)
Fan Fact: Bristol City hold the unenviable record of being the first team to be relegated three seasons in a row: they started in top tier of the Football League in the 1979–1980 season, and by the 1982–1983 season had plummeted to the bottom tier.
Best Pub for Away Fans: The Nova Scotia

BURNLEY

Nickname: The Clarets
Ground: Turf Moor, Burnley
Honours: Two League Championships; one FA Cup
Club Hero: Jimmy McIlroy – key midfielder in Burnley's 1959–1960 championship winning team; one of the stands at Turf Moor is named after him.
Biggest Win: Burnley 9 – Crystal Palace 0 (1909)
Biggest Defeat: Darwen 11 – Burnley 0 (1885)
Fan Fact: In the 1986–1987 season, Burnley came within one game of being relegated into the Football Conference; only a win on the last day of the season preserved their league status.
Best Pub for Away Fans: Burnley Cricket Club

CARDIFF CITY

Nickname: The Bluebirds
Ground: Cardiff City Stadium, Cardiff
Honours: One FA Cup; 22 Welsh Cups
Club Hero: Don Murray – talented defender who made over 400 appearances for Cardiff.
Biggest Win: Cardiff 16 – Knighton Town 0 (1961)
Biggest Defeat: Sheffield United 11 – Cardiff 2 (1926)
Fan Fact: Cardiff are the only non-English club to have won the FA Cup.
Best Pub for Away Fans: The Lansdowne Hotel

COVENTRY CITY

Nickname: The Sky Blues
Ground: Ricoh Arena, Coventry
Honours: One FA Cup
Club Hero: Steve Ogrizovic – goalkeeper who holds the record for most appearances for Coventry and also played in the 1987 FA Cup triumph.
Biggest Win: Coventry 9 – Bristol City 0 (1934)
Biggest Defeat: Norwich City 10 – Coventry 2 (1930)
Fan Fact: Coventry's old ground, Highfield Road, was the first all-seater stadium in England.
Best Pub for Away Fans: The Black Horse

CRYSTAL PALACE

Nickname: The Eagles
Ground: Selhurst Park, London
Honours: Two Tier Two titles
Club Hero: Jim Cannon – skilful Scottish defender who played for Palace for 16 years and spent 10 years as captain.
Biggest Win: Crystal Palace 9 – Barrow 0 (1959)
Biggest Defeat: Burnley 9 – Crystal Palace 0 (1909)
Fan Fact: Crystal Palace bought Ian Wright (who would go on to become one of Palace's greatest ever players) from amateur side Greenwich Borough, in exchange for a set of weights.
Best Pub for Away Fans: The Alliance

DERBY COUNTY

Nickname: The Rams
Ground: Pride Park, Derby
Honours: Two League Championships; one FA Cup
Club Hero: Brian Clough – inspirational and controversial manager who took Derby to their first ever league championship.
Biggest Win: Derby 12 – Finn Harps (Republic of Ireland) 0 (1976)
Biggest Defeat: Everton 11 – Derby 2 (1900)
Fan Fact: Derby striker Charlie George scored a hat-trick against Real Madrid in a European Cup tie that Derby won 4–1.
Best Pub for Away Fans: The Navigation

DONCASTER ROVERS

Nickname: The Rovers
Ground: Keepmoat Stadium, Doncaster
Honours: Three Tier Four titles
Club Hero: Alick Jeffrey – free-scoring Scottish forward who had two spells with the club in the 1950s and 1960s.
Biggest Win: Doncaster 10 – Darlington 0 (1964)
Biggest Defeat: Small Heath 12 – Doncaster 0 (1903)
Fan Fact: When the Rovers sold Harry Gregg to Manchester United in 1957 they received £23,000: the highest fee ever paid for a goalkeeper.
Best Pub for Away Fans: The Salutation

HULL CITY

Nickname: The Tigers
Ground: The KC Stadium, Hull
Honours: One Tier Three title
Club Hero: Ken Wagstaff – forward who scored 197 goals for the club in the 1960s and 1970s.
Biggest Win: Hull 11 – Carlisle United 1 (1939)
Biggest Defeat: Wolverhampton 8 – Hull 0 (1911)
Fan Fact: Hull were the first team to lose a penalty shoot-out; in 1970, Manchester United defeated them on penalties in the semi final of the Watney Mann Invitation Cup.
Best Pub for Away Fans: The Tap and Spile

IPSWICH TOWN

Nickname: The Tractor Boys
Ground: Portman Road, Ipswich
Honours: One League Championship; one FA Cup; one UEFA Cup
Club Hero: Bobby Robson – Ipswich's greatest manager who led them to FA Cup and UEFA Cup glory.
Biggest Win: Ipswich 11 – Cromer 0 (1936)
Biggest Defeat: Manchester United 9 – Ipswich 0 (1995)
Fan Fact: 1981 was a good year for Ipswich players: as well as winning the UEFA Cup, many of them also appeared in the film *Escape to Victory*, alongside Sylvester Stallone and Michael Caine.
Best Pub for Away Fans: The Station Hotel

LEEDS UNITED

Nickname: The Whites
Ground: Elland Road, Leeds
Honours: Three League Championships; one FA Cup; one League Cup; two Fairs Cups
Club Hero: Billy Bremner – combative and diminutive midfielder, and Leeds captain who was instrumental to the club's success in the late 1960s and early 1970s. A statue of Bremner stands outside Elland Road.
Biggest Win: Leeds 10 – FK Lyn (Norway) 0 (1969)
Biggest Defeat: Stoke City 8 – Leeds 1 (1934)
Fan Fact: The film *The Damned United* tells the story of Brian Clough's brief 44 day reign as manager of Leeds at the start of the 1974–1975 season.
Best Pub for Away Fans: The Drysalters

Half Time Quiz ⚽

Who was the last English manager to win the top division in England?

(Answer: Howard Wilkinson with Leeds United in the 1991–1992 season.)

LEICESTER CITY

Nickname: The Foxes
Ground: Walkers Stadium, Leicester
Honours: Three League Cups
Club Hero: Martin O'Neill – thoughtful and astute manager who led Leicester to two League Cup triumphs.
Biggest Win: Leicester 13 – Notts Olympic 0 (1894)
Biggest Defeat: Nottingham Forest 12 – Leicester 0 (1909)
Fan Fact: Leicester hold the unenviable record of most appearances in the FA Cup final (four) without winning the trophy.
Best Pub for Away Fans: The Leicester Gateway

MIDDLESBROUGH

Nickname: Boro
Ground: Riverside Stadium, Middlesbrough
Honours: One League Cup
Club Hero: Tony Mowbray – defender and captain who played a key role in helping Middlesbrough return to the top tier of English football in the late 1980s.
Biggest Win: Middlesbrough 9 – Brighton and Hove Albion 0 (1958)
Biggest Defeat: Blackburn Rovers 9 – Middlesbrough 0 (1954)
Fan Fact: Brian Clough became the fastest player to reach 100 league goals while playing for Middlesbrough.
Best Pub for Away Fans: Doctor Browns

MILLWALL

Nickname: The Lions
Ground: The New Den, London
Honours: One Tier Two; two Tier Three titles; one Tier Four title
Club Hero: Terry Hurlock – battling midfield player who was famous for his commitment to every game and to every tackle.
Biggest Win: Millwall 9 – Torquay United 1 (1927)
Biggest Defeat: Aston Villa 9 – Millwall 1 (1946)

Fan Fact: Until the 1960s, Millwall used to kick-off at 3.15pm on Saturday afternoons, rather than the common 3pm, in order to allow the dock-workers who made up a large proportion of Millwall's support to make it to matches after their morning shifts had finished.

Best Pub for Away Fans: The Shipwright Arms

NORWICH CITY

Nickname: The Canaries
Ground: Carrow Road, Norwich
Honours: Three Tier Two titles; two League Cups
Club Hero: Kevin Keelan – goalkeeper who holds the record for most appearances for Norwich. He played for the club during a period of relative success in the 1970s.
Biggest Win: Norwich 10 – Coventry City 2 (1930)
Biggest Defeat: Swindon Town 10 – Norwich 2 (1908)
Fan Fact: The 1975 League Cup final between Norwich and Aston Villa was the first final played at Wembley that involved two clubs from outside England's top division. Norwich lost 1–0.
Best Pub for Away Fans: The Compleat Angler

NOTTINGHAM FOREST

Nickname: Forest
Ground: The City Ground, Nottingham
Honours: One League Championship; two FA Cups; four League Cups; two European Cups; one European Super Cup
Club Hero: Brian Clough – motivational manager who led the club to their only league triumph and back-to-back European Cup victories.
Biggest Win: Clapton 0 – Nottingham Forest 14 (1891)
Biggest Defeat: Blackburn Rovers 9 – Nottingham Forest 1 (1937)
Fan Fact: Nottingham Forest are the only club in Europe to have won the European Cup (twice) more often than they have won their country's top league (once).
Best Pub for Away Fans: Larwood and Voce

PORTSMOUTH

Nickname: Pompey
Ground: Fratton Park, Portsmouth
Honours: Two League Championships; two FA Cups
Club Hero: Jimmy Dickinson – midfielder who holds the record for most appearances for Portsmouth. He was nicknamed 'Gentleman Jim' because he was never booked or sent off during his entire career.
Biggest Win: Portsmouth 9 – Notts County 1 (1927)
Biggest Defeat: Leicester 10 – Portsmouth 0 (1928)
Fan Fact: Field Marshal Bernard Montgomery was President of Portsmouth during the period when the club twice won the First Division.
Best Pub for Away Fans: Brewers Arms

PRESTON NORTH END

Nickname: The Lilywhites
Ground: Deepdale, Preston
Honours: Two League Championships; two FA Cups
Club Hero: Tom Finney – cultured forward who played for Preston for his entire career, scoring 187 league goals. Finney also gained 76 England caps and fought in the Western Desert during World War Two.
Biggest Win: Preston 26 – Hyde 0 (1887)
Biggest Defeat: Blackpool 7 – Preston 0 (1948)
Fan Fact: Preston became the first team to win the double, when they won the inaugural Football League title and the FA Cup in the 1888–1889 season.
Best Pub for Away Fans: The Hesketh Arms

QUEENS PARK RANGERS

Nickname: The Hoops
Ground: Loftus Road, London
Honours: One League Cup
Club Hero: Stan Bowles – midfielder who played during QPR's most successful spell in the 1970s, and was also known for his rather hectic personal life.

Biggest Win: QPR 9 – Tranmere Rovers 2 (1960)
Biggest Defeat: Manchester United 8 – QPR 1 (1969)
Fan Fact: QPR were the first club in England to install an artificial grass pitch. However, it did not last long as it proved unpopular with both players and fans.
Best Pub for Away Fans: The Central Bar

READING

Nickname: The Royals
Ground: Madejski Stadium, Reading
Honours: One Tier Two title; three Tier Three titles; one Tier Four title
Club Hero: Robin Friday – talented forward who was as renowned for his exploits off the pitch as his performances on it.
Biggest Win: Reading 10 – Crystal Palace 2 (1946)
Biggest Defeat: Preston 18 – Reading 0 (1894)
Fan Fact: Reading hold the record for most points gained in a single season in England; they amassed 106 points during their run to the 2005–2006 Championship title.
Best Pub for Away Fans: The Three Guineas

SCUNTHORPE UNITED

Nickname: The Iron
Ground: Glanford Park, Scunthorpe
Honours: One Tier Three title
Club Hero: Alex Calvo-Garcia – attack-minded midfielder who scored the memorable goal in the 1999 Division Three play-off that won the club promotion to Division Two.
Biggest Win: Scunthorpe 8 – Torquay United 1 (1995)
Biggest Defeat: Carlisle United 8 – Scunthorpe 0 (1952)
Fan Fact: Former England cricket captain Ian Botham played for Scunthorpe during 1980 in order to regain fitness after an injury.
Best Pub for Away Fans: The Berkeley

SHEFFIELD UNITED

Nickname: The Blades
Ground: Bramall Lane, Sheffield

Honours: One League Championship; four FA Cups
Club Hero: Tony Currie – midfielder with a high level of technical ability and a keen footballing eye. He played for the Blades for eight seasons during the late 1960s and early 1970s, becoming an England international.
Biggest Win: Sheffield United 10 – Burnley 0 (1929)
Biggest Defeat: Middlesbrough 10 – Sheffield United 3 (1933)
Fan Fact: Sheffield United bought a majority stake in a Chinese team in 2006 and changed their name to Chengdu Blades.
Best Pub for Away Fans: The Howard

SWANSEA CITY

Nickname: The Swans
Ground: Liberty Stadium, Swansea
Honours: One Tier Three title; one Tier Four title; 10 Welsh Cups
Club Hero: Ivor Allchurch – forward who was one of Wales' greatest players, played for Swansea in two different spells and scored 164 league goals. There is a statue of him outside the Liberty Stadium.
Biggest Win: Swansea 12 – Sliema Wanderers (Malta) 0 (1982)
Biggest Defeat: Liverpool 8 – Swansea 0 (1990)
Fan Fact: Swansea were the first Welsh club to play in the first round proper of the FA Cup.
Best Pub for Away Fans: The Bank Statement

WATFORD

Nickname: The Hornets
Ground: Vicarage Road, Watford
Honours: Two Tier Three titles; one Tier Four title
Club Hero: Graham Taylor – intelligent manager who presided over two periods of success at Watford. He took the team to the top tier of English football during both his spells in charge.
Biggest Win: Watford 10 – Lowestoft Town 1 (1926)
Biggest Defeat: Wolverhampton Wanderers 10 – Watford 0 (1912)

Fan Fact: In 2006, Malkay Mackay finally managed to play a match in the English Premier League with Watford; he had been promoted with both West Ham and Norwich but had been sold by both clubs before they started their Premier League campaigns.
Best Pub for Away Fans: The Odd Fellows

🥾 LEAGUE ONE 🥾

AFC BOURNEMOUTH

Nickname: The Cherries
Ground: Dean Court, Bournemouth
Honours: One Tier Three title
Club Hero: Harry Redknapp – manager who took the club into the second tier of English football and masterminded the FA Cup win over Manchester United in 1984, possibly the club's greatest victory.
Biggest Win: AFC Bournemouth 11 – Margate 0 (1971)
Biggest Defeat: Lincoln City 9 – AFC Bournemouth 0 (1982)
Fan Fact: Between 1923 and 1971, the club were known as Bournemouth and Boscombe Athletic Football Club, which was the longest name in the Football League.
Best Pub for Away Fans: Goat and Tricycle

BRENTFORD

Nickname: The Bees
Ground: Griffin Park, Brentford
Honours: One Tier Two title; two Tier Four titles
Club Hero: Dean Holdsworth – talented striker who was top-scorer for the club when they won the Third Division in the 1991–1992 season.
Biggest Win: Brentford 9 – Wrexham 0 (1963)
Biggest Defeat: Peterborough United 7 – Brentford 0 (2007)
Fan Fact: Fans visiting Griffin Park are spoiled for choice in terms of drinking establishments; there are pubs on all four corners of the ground.
Best Pub for Away Fans: The New Inn

BRIGHTON & HOVE ALBION

Nickname: The Seagulls
Ground: Withdean Stadium, Brighton
Honours: One Tier Three title; two Tier Four titles
Club Hero: Peter Ward – forward who had two spells with the club and scored less than a minute into his Brighton debut.
Biggest Win: Brighton & Hove Albion 10 – Wisbech 1 (1965)
Biggest Defeat: Middlesbrough 9 – Brighton & Hove Albion 0 (1958)
Fan Fact: The club are building a new stadium which should be ready for 2011. The current stadium, Withdean, is predominantly used as an athletics stadium and used to be a zoo.
Best Pub for Away Fans: The Evening Star

BRISTOL ROVERS

Nickname: The Pirates
Ground: Memorial Stadium, Bristol
Honours: One Tier Three title
Club Hero: Ian Holloway – charismatic midfielder who had three spells at the club as a player and went on to become the club's manager.
Biggest Win: Bristol Rovers 15 – Weymouth 1 (1900)
Biggest Defeat: Luton Town 12 – Bristol Rovers 0 (1936)
Fan Fact: In the 2001–2002 season, Bristol Rovers became the first team from the lowest tier of the Football League to defeat a Premier League team away from home when they won 3–1 against Derby County at Pride Park.
Best Pub for Away Fans: The Annexe Inn

CARLISLE UNITED

Nickname: The Blues
Ground: Brunton Park Stadium, Carlisle
Honours: One Tier Three title, two Tier Four titles
Club Hero: Jimmy Glass – goalkeeper who only played three games for the club, but whose last-minute winner against Plymouth Argyle in the last match of the 1998–1999 Third

Division season prevented Carlisle from being relegated out of the Football League.

Biggest Win: Carlisle 8 – Hartlepool United 0 (1928)

Biggest Defeat: Hull City 11 – Carlisle 1 (1939)

Fan Fact: Ivor Broadis became player-manager of Carlisle at the age of 23 in 1946; he remains the youngest person to have been player-manager of a club in the English Football League.

Best Pub for Away Fans: The Howard Arms

CHARLTON ATHLETIC

Nickname: The Addicks

Ground: The Valley, London

Honours: One FA Cup

Club Hero: Alan Curbishley – loyal midfielder who had two spells at the club as a player and went on to become Charlton manager, leading them to the Premier League.

Biggest Win: Charlton Athletic 8 – Middlesbrough 1 (1953)

Biggest Defeat: Aston Villa 11 – Charlton Athletic 1 (1959)

Fan Fact: Charlton were banned from playing matches at The Valley by the Football League due to safety failings in 1985 (forcing the club to share grounds first with Crystal Palace and later West Ham United), and did not return until 1992.

Best Pub for Away Fans: The Antigallaghan

COLCHESTER UNITED

Nickname: The U's

Ground: The Weston Homes Community Stadium, Colchester

Honours: One Football Conference title

Club Hero: Peter Wright – talented and tricky left winger who played for Colchester for 13 years, managing 99 goals.

Biggest Win: Colchester 9 – Bradford City 1 (1961)

Biggest Defeat: Leyton Orient 8 – Colchester 0 (1989)

Fan Fact: During a Colchester versus Millwall match in the 1980–1981 season, which Colchester won 3–0, a police sergeant attempted to arrest Millwall defender Mel Blyth for swearing.

Best Pub for Away Fans: The Norfolk

DAGENHAM AND REDBRIDGE

Nickname: The Daggers
Ground: Victoria Road, Dagenham
Honours: One Football Conference title
Club Hero: John Still – manager who led Dagenham to the Conference title in 2007, which took them into the Football League for the first time in their history.
Biggest Win: Dagenham 8 – Woking 1 (1994)
Biggest Defeat: Dagenham 0 – Hereford United 9 (2004)
Fan Fact: A series of mergers led to the creation of the modern-day club: first Leytonstone and Ilford merged in 1979; next came a merger with Walthamstow Avenue to create the new club Redbridge Forest. Finally Redbridge Forest merged with Dagenham to form Dagenham and Redbridge.
Best Pub for Away Fans: The Eastbrook

EXETER CITY

Nickname: The Grecians
Ground: St James Park, Exeter
Honours: One Tier Four title
Club Hero: Alan Banks – striker who had two spells with the club, during which he became Exeter's second highest goal scorer.
Biggest Win: Exeter 14 – Weymouth 0 (1908)
Biggest Defeat: Notts County 9 – Exeter 0 (1948)
Fan Fact: Exeter toured South America in 1914, playing against an early Brazil team.
Best Pub for Away Fans: The Wells Tavern

HARTLEPOOL UNITED

Nickname: Pools
Ground: Victoria Park, Hartlepool
Honours: Twice Tier Four runners-up
Club Hero: Keith Houchen – hugely talented forward who had two spells at the club as a player (during the first spell he was leading scorer four seasons in a row) and latterly became player-manager.

Biggest Win: Hartlepool 10 – Barrow 1 (1959)
Biggest Defeat: Wrexham 10 – Hartlepool 1 (1962)
Fan Fact: Hartlepool's mascot, H'Angus the Monkey, was elected mayor of Hartlepool in 2002 under the slogan 'Free bananas for schoolchildren'. He managed to gain re-election in 2005 with a majority of over 10,000, and in 2009 became the only directly elected mayor in Britain ever to win a third term.
Best Pub for Away Fans: The Corner Flag

HUDDERSFIELD TOWN

Nickname: The Terriers
Ground: Galpharm Stadium, Huddersfield
Honours: Three League Championships; one FA Cup
Club Hero: Herbert Chapman – hugely influential manager who led Huddersfield to their first major trophy, the FA Cup, and to two league championships.
Biggest Win: Huddersfield Town 10 – Blackpool 1 (1930)
Biggest Defeat: Manchester City 10 – Huddersfield Town 1 (1987)
Fan Fact: Between 1923 and 1926, Huddersfield became the first team in England to win the top league three seasons in a row.
Best Pub for Away Fans: Ricky's Bar

LEYTON ORIENT

Nickname: The O's
Ground: Brisbane Road, London
Honours: One Tier Three title
Club Hero: Peter Kitchen – forward who had two spells at the club, and who averaged just under a goal every two games. He helped Orient reach the semi finals of the FA Cup, their best ever performance in the competition.
Biggest Win: Leyton Orient 8 – Crystal Palace 0 (1955)
Biggest Defeat: Leyton Orient 0 – Aston Villa 8 (1929)
Fan Fact: Peter Shilton became the first player to play 1,000 league games while playing for Leyton Orient, in December 1996.
Best Pub for Away Fans: The Coach and Horses

Half Time Quiz ⚽

Who was the first player from outside the British Isles to captain an FA Cup winning side?

(Answer: Eric Cantona. He captained Manchester United in the 1996 FA Cup final.)

MILTON KEYNES DONS

Nickname: The Dons
Ground: StadiumMK, Milton Keynes
Honours: One Tier Four title
Club Hero: Paul Ince – manager who led the young club to its only major honour, the League Two title.
Biggest Win: MK Dons 5 – Accrington Stanley 0 (2007)
Biggest Defeat: Huddersfield 5 – MK Dons 0 (2006)
Fan Fact: The club were originally known as Wimbledon FC but changed their name after moving to Milton Keynes from south-west London. This move proved unpopular with many fans and they responded by setting up a new club, AFC Wimbledon, who currently play in the non-league pyramid.
Best Pub for Away Fans: The Beacon

NOTTS COUNTY

Nickname: The Magpies
Ground: Meadow Lane, Nottingham
Honours: Three Tier Two titles; three Tier Four titles; one FA Cup
Club Hero: Jimmy Sirrel – manager who led the club for two periods, and took them back into the top tier of English football in 1981. A stand at Meadow Lane is named in his honour.
Biggest Win: Notts County 15 – Rotherham Town 0 (1885)
Biggest Defeat: Blackburn Rovers 9 – Notts County 1 (1889)
Fan Fact: Notts County are the oldest fully professional football club in the world, having been formed in 1862.
Best Pub for Away Fans: The Globe

OLDHAM ATHLETIC

Nickname: The Latics
Ground: Boundary Park, Oldham
Honours: One Tier Two title; one Tier Three title
Club Hero: Andy Ritchie – forward who had two spells at the club and went on to become manager. He played a key role during Oldham's successful 1989–1990 season, during which they reached the semi final of the FA Cup and the final of the League Cup.
Biggest Win: Oldham 11 – Southport 0 (1962)
Biggest Defeat: Tranmere Rovers 13 – Oldham 4 (1935)
Fan Fact: The club were originally known as Pine Villa; the name Oldham Athletic was adopted in 1899.
Best Pub for Away Fans: The Old Grey Mare

PETERBOROUGH UNITED

Nickname: The Posh
Ground: London Road Stadium, Peterborough
Honours: Two Tier Four titles
Club Hero: Terrence Bly – lethal forward who scored 52 goals during Peterborough's debut season in the football league.
Biggest Win: Barnet 1 – Peterborough 9 (1998)
Biggest Defeat: Tranmere Rovers 7 – Peterborough 0 (1985)
Fan Fact: Peterborough scored 134 goals in the 1960–1961 season, which remains the largest number of goals scored by a team in England in one season.
Best Pub for Away Fans: The Palmerston Arms

PLYMOUTH ARGYLE

Nickname: The Pilgrims
Ground: Home Park, Plymouth
Honours: Two Tier Three titles; one Tier Four title
Club Hero: Kevin Hodges – tricky winger who holds the record for most appearances for Plymouth, and who helped them reach the semi final of the FA Cup in 1984.
Biggest Win: Plymouth 8 – Millwall 1 (1932)
Biggest Defeat: Stoke City 9 – Plymouth 0 (1960)

Fan Fact: In 1973 Plymouth defeated Brazilian club Santos, who boasted Pelé in their starting line-up, 3–2 in a friendly match.
Best Pub for Away Fans: The Britannia Inn

ROCHDALE

Nickname: The Dale
Ground: Spotland Stadium, Rochdale
Honours: Two Lancashire Combination League titles
Club Hero: Reg Jenkins – powerful forward who helped the club gain promotion to the Third Division in 1969.
Biggest Win: Rochdale 8 – Chesterfield 1 (1926)
Biggest Defeat: Wrexham 8 – Rochdale 0 (1929)
Fan Fact: Rochdale are the only club to reach a major cup final in England while playing in the bottom tier of the Football League. They achieved this feat in 1962 when they reached the League Cup final, where they lost 4–0 to Norwich City over two legs.
Best Pub for Away Fans: The Church Inn

SHEFFIELD WEDNESDAY

Nickname: The Owls
Ground: Hillsborough, Sheffield
Honours: Four League Championships; three FA Cups; one League Cup
Club Hero: John Fantham – Wednesday's leading goal scorer in the post-war period, who helped them reach second place in the league in the 1960–1961 season.
Biggest Win: Sheffield Wednesday 12 – Halliwell 0 (1891)
Biggest Defeat: Aston Villa 10 – Sheffield Wednesday 0 (1912)
Fan Fact: Sheffield Wednesday were originally a cricket club. They acquired the peculiar name 'Wednesday' because that was when they played their matches.
Best Pub for Away Fans: The New Barrack Tavern

SOUTHAMPTON

Nickname: The Saints
Ground: St Mary's Stadium, Southampton

Honours: One Tier Three title; one FA Cup
Club Hero: Matthew Le Tissier – technically gifted midfielder who played for Southampton for his entire career and, impressively for a midfielder, is the club's second highest scorer.
Biggest Win: Southampton 14 – Newbury 0 (1894)
Biggest Defeat: Everton 8 – Southampton 0 (1971)
Fan Fact: Manchester United famously changed shirts during half time when losing 3–0 against Southampton at their old ground, the Dell. United manager Alex Ferguson blamed the poor performance on the difficulty his players were experiencing in picking out teammates in their grey strips. Southampton won the match 3–1.
Best Pub for Away Fans: The Admiral Sir Lucius Curtis

SWINDON TOWN

Nickname: The Robins
Ground: The County Ground, Swindon
Honours: Two Tier Four titles; one League Cup
Club Hero: Don Rogers – versatile winger who had two spells with the Robins, and whose two goals in extra time in the 1969 League Cup final gave the club a 3–1 victory over Arsenal – and their only major trophy.
Biggest Win: Farnham United Breweries 1 – Swindon 10 (1925)
Biggest Defeat: Man City 10 – Swindon 1 (1930)
Fan Fact: During the 1993–1994 Premier League season, Swindon finished bottom of the league and conceded 100 goals. This remains the highest number of goals conceded in one Premier League season.
Best Pub for Away Fans: The Merlin

TRANMERE ROVERS

Nickname: Super Whites
Ground: Prenton Park, Birkenhead
Honours: One Football League Trophy
Club Hero: John Aldridge – Irish forward who made his debut for Tranmere aged 32, but still went on to play for the club for a

further seven years, helping them to reach the First Division play-offs three years in a row. He scored 170 goals, making him the club's second highest goal scorer.

Biggest Win: Tranmere 13 – Oswestry United 0 (1914)

Biggest Defeat: Tottenham 9 – Tranmere 1 (1953)

Fan Fact: The satirical rock band, Half Man Half Biscuit, are such devout followers of Tranmere Rovers that they once turned down the offer to appear on Channel 4 because the club were playing a match at the time when they would have been filming.

Best Pub for Away Fans: The Swan

WALSALL

Nickname: The Saddlers

Ground: The Bescot Stadium, Walsall

Honours: Two Tier Four titles

Club Hero: James Walker – small but talented goalkeeper who played for Walsall for 11 years, making 475 appearances and helping the club achieve promotion on three separate occasions.

Biggest Win: Walsall 10 – Darwen 0 (1899)

Biggest Defeat: Birmingham City 12 – Walsall 0 (1892)

Fan Fact: Walsall produced one of the greatest FA Cup shocks in history when they defeated Arsenal, who would go on to be English champions for the next three seasons, 2–0 in January 1933.

Best Pub for Away Fans: The King George V

YEOVIL TOWN

Nickname: The Glovers

Ground: Huish Park, Yeovil

Honours: One Tier Four title; one Football Conference title

Club Hero: Warren Patmore – prolific striker who played for the club for six years, scoring over 100 league goals.

Biggest Win: Yeovil 10 – Kidderminster Harriers 0 (1955)

Biggest Defeat: Manchester United 8 – Yeovil 0 (1949)

Fan Fact: Yeovil's rather peculiar nickname derives from the fact that the town was historically associated with glove-making.

Best Pub for Away Fans: The Bell

👟 LEAGUE TWO 👟

ACCRINGTON STANLEY

Nickname: Stanley
Ground: Crown Ground, Accrington
Honours: One Football Conference title
Club Hero: Eric Whalley – chairman who oversaw huge improvements at the club, both on and off the pitch: building new stands and helping to guide the club back into the Football League.
Biggest Win: Accrington 10 – Lincoln United 1 (1999)
Biggest Defeat: Runcorn 9 – Accrington 1 (1985)
Fan Fact: The club went out of business in the 1960s and was revived in 1968 after a meeting at the town library.

ALDERSHOT TOWN

Nickname: The Shots
Ground: Recreation Ground, Aldershot
Honours: One Football Conference title
Club Hero: Nikki Bull – talented goalkeeper who played for the club for seven years, helping them win promotion to the Football League in 2008.
Biggest Win: Aldershot 8 – Bishops Stortford 0 (1998)
Biggest Defeat: Worthing 6 – Aldershot 0 (1999)
Fan Fact: Aldershot Town replaced the town's old club, Aldershot FC, who went out of business during the 1991–1992 season.

BARNET

Nickname: The Bees
Ground: Underhill Stadium, Barnet
Honours: Two Football Conference titles
Club Hero: Barry Fry – manager who managed to guide Barnet to promotion to the third tier in English football in the 1992–1993 season, despite huge financial problems and a highly unsettled relationship with the club's chairman.

Biggest Win: Barnet 7 – Blackpool 0 (2000)
Biggest Defeat: Peterborough United 9 – Barnet 1 (1998)
Fan Fact: Former Barnet chairman Stan Flashman sacked manager Barry Fry on eight separate occasions. Each time he was re-instated.

BRADFORD CITY

Nickname: The Bantams
Ground: Valley Parade, Bradford
Honours: One Tier Two title; one Tier Three title; one FA Cup
Club Hero: Stuart McCall – tough but talented midfielder who had two spells with the club and went on to become manager. Was club captain when the club achieved promotion to the Premier League in the 1998–1999 season, and famously fell off a car roof while celebrating this success.
Biggest Win: Bradford 11 – Rotherham United 1 (1928)
Biggest Defeat: Man City 8 – Bradford 0 (1927)
Fan Fact: Club scarves have sold well in recent years, mainly because the Bantams' colours are the same as those of Gryffindor: Harry Potter's house in the famous series of books.

BURTON ALBION

Nickname: The Brewers
Ground: Pirelli Stadium, Burton-on-Trent
Honours: One Football Conference title
Club Hero: Nigel Clough – manager who led the club into the Football Conference and achieved one of the club's greatest ever results (and one of the FA Cup's greatest shocks), by holding Manchester United to a 0–0 draw in the third round of the competition in 2006.
Biggest Win: Burton 12 – Coalville Town 1 (1954)
Biggest Defeat: Barnet 10 – Burton 0 (1970)
Fan Fact: Burton Albion are the latest in a long line of football clubs from the town: Burton Swifts, Burton Wanderers and Burton United enjoyed a brief existence prior to the First World War.

BURY

Nickname: The Shakers
Ground: Gigg Lane, Bury
Honours: One Tier Two title; two Tier Three titles; two FA Cups
Club Hero: Craig Madden – free-scoring forward whose goals helped the club gain promotion to the Third Division in 1984–1985. Madden still holds the record for most goals scored in a single season for Bury.
Biggest Win: Bury 12 – Stockton 1 (1897)
Biggest Defeat: Blackburn Rovers 10 – Bury 0 (1887)
Fan Fact: Captain of the Indian national team, Baichung Bhutia, became the first Indian footballer to play professionally in Europe when he signed for Bury in 1999.

CHELTENHAM TOWN

Nickname: The Robins
Ground: Abbey Business Stadium, Cheltenham
Honours: One Football Conference title
Club Hero: Steve Cotterill – hugely successful manager who achieved three promotions with the club, taking them from the Southern Football League Premier Division into the Nationwide Division Two (now known as League One) in the 2001–2002 season. Cotterill also masterminded an FA Cup campaign that saw the Robins reach the fifth round – the furthest the club had ever progressed in the competition.
Biggest Win: Cheltenham 12 – Chippenham Rovers 0 (1935)
Biggest Defeat: Merthyr Tydfil 10 – Cheltenham 1 (1952)
Fan Fact: Gloucester City will become tenants at the Abbey Business Stadium in season 2010–2011 while flood damage at their ground is repaired. They will be the third tenants that Cheltenham have had in the past 20 years, the others being St Marks CA and Endsleigh FC.

CHESTERFIELD

Nickname: The Spireites
Ground: The Recreation Ground, Chesterfield
Honours: Two Tier Four titles

Club Hero: Jamie Hewitt – defender who had two spells at the club, playing over 500 games. He famously scored the equaliser in the 1997 FA Cup semi final against Middlesbrough in the last minute of extra time, to force a replay.

Biggest Win: Chesterfield 10 – Glossop 0 (1903)

Biggest Defeat: Gillingham 10 – Chesterfield 0 (1987)

Fan Fact: The Recreation Ground, also known as Saltergate, is one of the oldest football grounds in the world: the first game was played there in 1871.

CREWE ALEXANDRA

Nickname: The Railwaymen

Ground: Alexandra Stadium, Crewe

Honours: Two Welsh Cups

Club Hero: Seth Johnson – midfielder who only played for Crewe for three years, but permanently endeared himself to the club's fans by delaying his big move to Derby in order to help Crewe in their relegation fight in 1999. His performances in the last months of the season helped the club keep their place in the second tier of English football.

Biggest Win: Crewe 8 – Rotherham 0 (1932)

Biggest Defeat: Tottenham 13 – Crewe 2 (1960)

Fan Fact: Dario Gradi managed the club for a 24 year spell between 1983 and 2007. He returned as caretaker manager in 2008 and again in 2009.

GILLINGHAM

Nickname: The Gills

Ground: KRBS Priestfield Stadium, Gillingham

Honours: One Tier Four title

Club Hero: Tony Cascarino – powerful centre forward who played for Gillingham for seven years before moving on to enjoy success at Aston Villa, Chelsea, Marseille, and AS Nancy.

Biggest Win: Gillingham 12 – Gloucester City 1 (1946)

Biggest Defeat: Luton Town 8 – Gillingham 0 (1929)

Fan Fact: Republic of Ireland legend, Tony Cascarino, moved from non-league side Crockenhill to Gillingham in exchange for training equipment and a set of tracksuits.

Half Time Quiz ☉

How many teams have won the 'double' (winning the League and the FA Cup in the same season) in England?

(Answer: Seven – Arsenal (1970–1971, 1997–1998 and 2001–2002); Aston Villa (1896–1897); Chelsea (2009–2010); Liverpool (1985–1986); Manchester United (1993–1994, 1995–1996 and 1998–1999); Preston North End (1888–1889); and Tottenham Hotspur (1960–1961).)

HEREFORD UNITED

Nickname: The Bulls
Ground: Edgar Street, Hereford
Honours: One Tier Three title; one Welsh Cup
Club Hero: Mel Pejic – consistent defender who played for Hereford for 12 years and went on to become the club's captain.
Biggest Win: Hereford 11 – Thynnes Athletic 0 (1947)
Biggest Defeat: Middlesbrough 7 – Hereford 0 (1996)
Fan Fact: Hereford hold the record for the biggest victory by a non-league club over a league club in the FA Cup; during the 1957–1958 season they defeated Queens Park Rangers 6–1.

LINCOLN CITY

Nickname: The Red Imps
Ground: Sincil Bank, Lincoln
Honours: One Tier Four title; one Football Conference title
Club Hero: Graham Taylor – defender and then manager who led the club to the Fourth Division title in 1976, gaining a record points total.
Biggest Win: Peterborough United 0 – Lincoln 13 (1895)
Biggest Defeat: Man City 11 – Lincoln 3 (1895)
Fan Fact: Lincoln have played the greatest number of seasons in the Football League without ever reaching England's top tier.

MACCLESFIELD TOWN

Nickname: The Silkmen
Ground: Moss Rose, Macclesfield
Honours: Two Football Conference titles
Club Hero: John Askey – prolific forward who helped the club win two Football Conference titles, and was a key part of the team that gained promotion to the third tier of the Football League.
Biggest Win: Macclesfield Town 9 – Hartford St Johns 0 (1884)
Biggest Defeat: Davenham 8 – Macclesfield Town 1 (1885)
Fan Fact: Macclesfield won the Football Conference in the 1994–1995 season, but were denied promotion to the Football League because their ground did not meet the required criteria. Two seasons later they won the League again and by this time the ground had been upgraded, so they were able to take their place in the fourth tier of English football.

MORECAMBE

Nickname: The Shrimps
Ground: Christie Park, Morecambe (the Globe Arena from 2010–2011 season)
Honours: One FA Trophy
Club Hero: Sammy McIlroy – manager who led the club to the Football League for the first time in their history, after winning the Conference Play-off final in 2007.
Biggest Win: Morecambe 7 – Altrincham 0 (1996)
Biggest Defeat: Leek Town 7 – Morecambe 0 (1998)
Fan Fact: Sammy McIlroy and his predecessor as club manager Jim Harvey, used to be good friends but fell out when Harvey was sacked and replaced by McIlroy.

NORTHAMPTON TOWN

Nickname: The Cobblers
Ground: Sixfields Stadium, Northampton
Honours: One Tier Three title; one Tier Four title
Club Hero: Dave Bowen – manager who took the club from the bottom tier of the Football League to the top tier in the 1960s. The north stand at Sixfields is named after him.

Biggest Win: Northampton 10 – Sutton United 0 (1907)
Biggest Defeat: Southampton 11 – Northampton 0 (1901)
Fan Fact: The club finished bottom of the fourth tier of the Football League in the 1993–1994 season, but avoided being relegated to the Football Conference because the team that would have replaced them, Kidderminster Harriers, did not meet the stadium criteria for playing in the Football League.

OXFORD UNITED

Nickname: The Yellows
Ground: Kassam Stadium, Oxford
Honours: One Tier Two title; two Tier Three titles; one League Cup
Club Hero: John Aldridge – talented Irish forward who played for the club during their successful spell in the 1980s, helping them gain promotion to England's top league and win the League Cup.
Biggest Win: Oxford 9 – Dorchester Town 1 (1995)
Biggest Defeat: Sunderland 7 – Oxford 0 (1998)
Fan Fact: Oxford should have qualified for the UEFA Cup after winning the 1986 English League Cup. Unfortunately for the club, English teams were banned from Europe at this time due to sanctions imposed after the Heysel Disaster.

PORT VALE

Nickname: The Valiants
Ground: Vale Park, Burslem
Honours: One Tier Four title
Club Hero: John Rudge – manager who led the club for 16 years and took them to the second tier in the Football League.
Biggest Win: Port Vale 9 – Chesterfield 1 (1932)
Biggest Defeat: Sheffield United 10 – Port Vale 0 (1892)
Fan Fact: Famous supporter, singer Robbie Williams, agreed to record a song for the computer game FIFA 2000 on the condition that Port Vale were included in the game.

ROTHERHAM UNITED

Nickname: The Millers
Ground: Don Valley Stadium, Rotherham

Honours: One Tier Three title; one Tier Four title

Club Hero: Ronnie Moore – prolific forward who was with the club for three seasons, and played an influential role in the side that won the 1980–1981 Division Three title. Moore returned to the club in 1997 as manager, leading them to the giddy heights of England's second tier.

Biggest Win: Rotherham 8 – Oldham Athletic 0 (1947)

Biggest Defeat: Bradford City 11 – Rotherham 1 (1928)

Fan Fact: The Chuckle Brothers, stars of the BBC children's programme *Chucklevision*, were appointed honorary presidents of the club in 2007.

SHREWSBURY TOWN

Nickname: The Shrews

Ground: The Greenhous Meadow Stadium, Shrewsbury

Honours: One Tier Three title; one Tier Four title

Club Hero: Graham Turner – manager who led the club to the Third Division title and two FA Cup quarter finals in the late 1970s and early 1980s.

Biggest Win: Shrewsbury 7 – Swindon Town 0 (1955)

Biggest Defeat: Coventry City 8 – Shrewsbury 1 (1963)

Fan Fact: The club have had five different grounds over their long history, moving to their current home at the Prostar Stadium in 2007.

SOUTHEND UNITED

Nickname: The Blues

Ground: Roots Hall, Southend-on-Sea

Honours: One Tier Three title; one Tier Four title

Club Hero: Chris Powell – skilful defender who played for the club for six years and went on to play for England.

Biggest Win: Southend 10 – Aldershot 1 (1990)

Biggest Defeat: Brighton and Hove Albion 9 – Southend 1 (1965)

Fan Fact: Southend managed to avoid suffering the ignominy of being relegated until 1966, when they were demoted from the Third Division.

STEVENAGE BOROUGH

Nickname: The Boro
Ground: Broadhall Way, Stevenage
Honours: Two Football Conference titles
Club Hero: Mark Gittings – forward who played for the club for 15 years, and is Stevenage's record goal scorer.
Biggest Win: Runcorn Halton 0 – Stevenage 8 (1995)
Biggest Defeat: Farnborough 6 – Stevenage 1 (2002)
Fan Fact: Stevenage won the Football Conference in the 1995–1996 season, but were denied a place in the Football League because their ground did not fulfil the criteria required by the League.

STOCKPORT COUNTY

Nickname: The Hatters
Ground: Edgeley Park, Stockport
Honours: One Tier Four title
Club Hero: Kevin Francis – tall but skilful forward who had two spells at the club and was the club's top scorer two seasons in a row.
Biggest Win: Stockport 13 – Halifax Town 0 (1934)
Biggest Defeat: Stockport 0 – Sheffield Wednesday 7 (1986)
Fan Fact: Stockport are perhaps the only club in Britain to have changed their kit due to a clash with a nation Britain was at war with; the kit Stockport wore at the outbreak of the Falklands War in 1982 was very similar to that used by the Argentina national team.

TORQUAY UNITED

Nickname: The Gulls
Ground: Plainmoor, Torquay
Honours: One Southern League title
Club Hero: Derek Dawkins – midfielder who played for the club during the 1980s, and who famously scored the winning goal in a League Cup match against a star-studded Tottenham side in 1987.
Biggest Win: Torquay 9 – Swindon Town 0 (1952)

Biggest Defeat: Fulham 10 – Torquay 2 (1931)
Fan Fact: In 1910, Torquay United and Ellacombe merged to form Torquay Town. Ten years later, Torquay Town merged with local rivals Babbacombe, adopted the name Torquay United and the modern club was born.

WYCOMBE WANDERERS

Nickname: The Blues
Ground: Adams Park, High Wycombe
Honours: One Football Conference title
Club Hero: Steve Brown – midfielder who played for the club for a decade and was an influential member of the side that reached the FA Cup semi final in 2001.
Biggest Win: Wycombe 6 – Telford United 1 (1991)
Biggest Defeat: Wycombe 0 – Shrewsbury Town 7 (2008)
Fan Fact: Roy Essandoh was signed by Wycombe after the club broadcast an appeal for strikers on Ceefax due to an injury crisis. He came on as a substitute in the FA Cup quarter final against Leicester City in 2001 and scored the winning goal.

🥾 NON-LEAGUE 🥾

AFC WIMBLEDON

Nickname: The Dons
Ground: Kingsmeadow, Kingston upon Thames
Honours: One Conference South title; one Isthmian League Division One title
Club Hero: Terry Brown – manager who led the club to back-to-back promotions from the Isthmian League to the Football Conference.
Biggest Win: AFC Wimbledon 9 – Slough Town 0 (2007)
Biggest Defeat: York City 5 – AFC Wimbledon 0 (2010)
Fan Fact: AFC Wimbledon were formed by fans of the original Wimbledon FC, after the club was moved to Milton Keynes. Their run of 78 league games in a row without defeat is an English record.

DARLINGTON

Nickname: The Quakers
Ground: The Northern Echo Darlington Arena, Darlington
Honours: One Tier Four title; one Football Conference title
Club Hero: Craig Liddle – committed defender who played for the club for seven years and went on to become club captain.
Biggest Win: Darlington 13 – Scarborough 1 (1891)
Biggest Defeat: Doncaster Rovers 10 – Darlington 0 (1964)
Fan Fact: In the 1999–2000 season, Manchester United withdrew from the FA Cup to play in the Club World Cup, and this left an uneven number of teams in the third round. A draw was made of all the losing teams in the second round and Darlington were the lucky club, although their luck did not last long as they lost 2–1 to Aston Villa in the third round tie.

EBBSFLEET UNITED

Nickname: The Fleet
Ground: Stonebridge Road, Northfleet
Honours: One Isthmian League Premier Division title; one FA Trophy
Club Hero: Liam Daish – manager who led the club to victory in the 2008 FA Trophy final at Wembley.
Biggest Win: Ebbsfleet United 8 – Clacton Town 1 (1962)
Biggest Defeat: Bournemouth 7 – Ebbsfleet United 0 (1964)
Fan Fact: Ebbsfleet United are owned by an internet-based company, whose members get to control the club by voting on decisions that the club has to make – from major issues such as accepting transfer bids, to minor issues such as deciding what food the club will sell at the ground.

FC UNITED OF MANCHESTER

Nickname: Red Rebels
Ground: Gigg Lane, Bury
Honours: One North West Counties League Division One title; one North West Counties League Division Two title
Club Hero: Karl Marginson – manager who has led the club since its formation and masterminded three promotions in the club's first three years.

Biggest Win: FC United 10 – Castleton Gabriels 2 (2005)
Biggest Defeat: FC United 1 – Bradford Park Avenue 5 (2010)
Fan Fact: The club was formed in June 2005 by Manchester United fans who were angered by the take-over of their club by the Glazer family.

GRIMSBY TOWN

Nickname: The Mariners
Ground: Blundell Park, Cleethorpes
Honours: Two Tier Two titles; one Tier Three title; one Tier Four title
Club Hero: Ivano Bonetti – talented and controversial Italian midfielder who only spent one season with the club, but became a Grimsby legend after paying his own transfer fee and putting in some star performances. Famously left after manager Brian Laws threw a plate of chicken at him.
Biggest Win: Grimsby 8 – Tranmere Rovers 0 (1925)
Biggest Defeat: Arsenal 9 – Grimsby 1 (1931)
Fan Fact: Grimsby have suffered a calamitous slide down the leagues in the past decade: in the 1998–1999 season they finished 11th in England's second tier; by 2009–2010 they had plummeted to 23rd in the fourth tier and were relegated to the Conference National.

LUTON TOWN

Nickname: The Hatters
Ground: Kenilworth Road, Luton
Honours: One Tier Two title; one Tier Three title; one Tier Four title; one League Cup
Club Hero: Mick Harford – tough and skilful forward who had two spells with the club and was part of the 1988 League Cup winning side.
Biggest Win: Luton 15 – Great Yarmouth Town 0 (1914)
Biggest Defeat: Birmingham City 9 – Luton 0 (1898)
Fan Fact: Luton player Joe Payne still holds the record for most goals in a single match; he scored 10 goals against Bristol Rovers in 1936.

RUSHDEN AND DIAMONDS

Nickname: The Diamonds
Ground: Nene Park, Irthlingborough
Honours: One Tier Four title; one Football Conference title
Club Hero: Paul Underwood – defender who played for the club for seven years, and was club captain when Rushden won both the Football Conference title and the Football League Third Division title.
Biggest Win: Rushden 7 – Redditch United 0 (1994)
Biggest Defeat: Cardiff City 7 – Rushden 1 (2001)
Fan Fact: The club has its own radio station, Radio Diamonds, which broadcasts on the day of home matches.

YORK CITY

Nickname: The Minstermen
Ground: Bootham Crescent, York
Honours: One Tier Four title
Club Hero: Arthur Bottom – prolific forward who was a key member of the York team that reached the FA Cup semi finals in 1955, and is also the club's joint record holder for most goals in a season.
Biggest Win: York 9 – Southport 1 (1957)
Biggest Defeat: Chester City 12 – York 0 (1936)
Fan Fact: In the penalty shoot-out at the end of the 2009 FA Trophy quarter final between York and Kidderminster Harriers, a record 25 consecutive penalties were scored before Kidderminster missed their 13th penalty and York won the shoot-out 13–12.

👟 SCOTTISH CLUBS 👟

ABERDEEN

Nickname: The Dons
Ground: Pittodrie Stadium, Aberdeen
Honours: Four League Championships; seven Scottish Cups; five Scottish League Cups; one European Cup Winners' Cup; one European Super Cup

Club Hero: Willie Miller – talented defender who played for the club for 18 years in the 1970s and 1980s, helping them win a host of trophies including the Cup Winners' Cup, three league titles and four Scottish Cups. He remains holder of the record for most appearances for Aberdeen and went on to manage the club in the early 1990s.

Biggest Win: Aberdeen 13 – Peterhead 0 (1932)

Biggest Defeat: Celtic 8 – Aberdeen 0 (1965)

Fan Fact: In the 1920s, Pittodrie became the first ground to introduce dugouts.

Best Pub for Away Fans: The Saltoun

CELTIC

Nickname: The Bhoys

Ground: Celtic Park, Glasgow

Honours: 42 League Championships; 34 Scottish Cups; 14 Scottish League Cups; one European Cup

Club Hero: Jock Stein – one of Britain's finest managers, who ended Celtic's long run without a trophy in 1965 and led them to their greatest triumph, the 1967 European Cup.

Biggest Win: Celtic 11 – Dundee 0 (1895)

Biggest Defeat: Motherwell 8 – Celtic 0 (1937)

Fan Fact: When Celtic won the European Cup in 1967, all 11 of the players (who became known as the Lisbon Lions) came from within a 30 mile radius of Celtic Park.

Best Pub for Away Fans: The Crystal Palace

DUNDEE UNITED

Nickname: The Terrors

Ground: Tannadice Park, Dundee

Honours: One League Championship; two Scottish Cups; two Scottish League Cups

Club Hero: Jim McLean – intelligent manager who managed the club for 22 years, taking them to their first Scottish Cup Final, their first league championship and perhaps most impressively, to the semi finals of the European Cup and the final of the UEFA Cup.

Biggest Win: Dundee United 14 – Nithsdale Wanderers 0 (1931)
Biggest Defeat: Motherwell 12 – Dundee United 1 (1954)
Fan Fact: Dundee United have a 100% record against European giants Barcelona; the club have been drawn against the Spaniards twice in European competition and were victorious in all four of the matches. (European ties are played over two legs.)
Best Pub for Away Fans: The Centenary Bar

HAMILTON ACADEMICAL

Nickname: The Accies
Ground: New Douglas Park, Hamilton
Honours: Four Tier Two titles
Club Hero: John McNaught – high scoring defender who had two spells at the club and helped Hamilton win the First Division title in 1986.
Biggest Win: Hamilton 11 – Chryston 1 (1885)
Biggest Defeat: Hibernian 11 – Hamilton 1 (1965)
Fan Fact: In 1971, Hamilton became the first club to sign players from behind the Iron Curtain when they recruited three players from Poland.
Best Pub for Away Fans: The Chambers Bar

HEART OF MIDLOTHIAN

Nickname: The Jambos
Ground: Tynecastle Stadium, Edinburgh
Honours: Four League Championships; seven Scottish Cups; four Scottish League Cups
Club Hero: John Robertson – powerful forward who had two spells at the club and was particularly famous for scoring against the club's main rivals, Hibernian.
Biggest Win: Hearts 21 – Anchor 0 (1880)
Biggest Defeat: Vale of Leven 8 – Hearts 1 (1883)
Fan Fact: Hearts managed to avoid being relegated until 1977, when they were demoted to the Second Division.
Best Pub for Away Fans: The Station Bar

Half Time Quiz ☻

Who is the only player to be brought on as a substitute for his own father?

(Answer: Eider Gudjohnsen, who came on for his father, Arnor, during an Iceland versus Latvia friendly in 1996.)

HIBERNIAN

Nickname: Hibs
Ground: Easter Road, Edinburgh
Honours: Four League Championships; two Scottish Cups; three Scottish League Cups
Club Hero: Eddie Turnbull – talented striker who was a member of the 'Famous Five' forward line that played for Hibs in the 1950s, helping them to win three league titles during that period. Turnbull was also the first British player to score in a European competition.
Biggest Win: Hibernian 15 – Peebles Rovers 1 (1961)
Biggest Defeat: Rangers 10 – Hibernian 0 (1898)
Fan Fact: Hibernian were the first British club to play in Europe; they took part in the inaugural European Cup in 1955.
Best Pub for Away Fans: The Four in Hand

INVERNESS CALEDONIAN THISTLE

Nickname: Caley Thistle
Ground: Caledonian Stadium, Inverness
Honours: Two Tier Two titles; one Tier Four title; one Scottish Challenge Cup
Club Hero: Jimmy Calder – Calder played as both a striker and goalkeeper for the club. He was a forward until a serious knee injury forced him to give up playing outfield, but rather than retire from football, he decided to become a goalkeeper and played in Inverness' famous 3–1 win over Celtic at Celtic Park in 2000.
Biggest Win: Inverness 8 – Annan Athletic 1 (1996)
Biggest Defeat: Airdrieonians 6 – Inverness 0 (2001)

Fan Fact: The famous *Sun* newspaper headline, 'Super Caley Go Ballistic Celtic Are Atrocious' that came after the Scottish Cup victory in 2000, is framed in the foyer of the club's stadium.
Best Pub for Away Fans: The Phoenix

KILMARNOCK

Nickname: Kille
Ground: Rugby Park, Kilmarnock
Honours: One League Championship; three Scottish Cups
Club Hero: Willie Waddell – manager who led Kilmarnock to their only league championship in 1965.
Biggest Win: Kilmarnock 11 – Paisley Academicals 1 (1930)
Biggest Defeat: Celtic 9 – Kilmarnock 1 (1938)
Fan Fact: Kilmarnock's victory over Falkirk in the 1997 Scottish Cup Final was the first Scottish Cup Final since 1957 not to feature a club from one of Scotland's four cities. Interestingly, the 1957 final also featured Kilmarnock and Falkirk.
Best Pub for Away Fans: The Howard Arms

MOTHERWELL

Nickname: The Steelmen
Ground: Fir Park, Motherwell
Honours: One League Championship; two Scottish Cups; one Scottish League Cup
Club Hero: Tom Boyd – defender who played for the club for eight years and captained the team that won the Scottish Cup in 1991.
Biggest Win: Motherwell 12 – Dundee United 1 (1954)
Biggest Defeat: Aberdeen 8 – Motherwell 0 (1979)
Fan Fact: Willie MacFadyen scored 52 goals to help Motherwell win the league championship in the 1931–1932 season. This remains a Scottish record.
Best Pub for Away Fans: The Jack Daniels Bar

RANGERS

Nickname: The Gers
Ground: Ibrox Stadium, Glasgow

Honours: 53 League Championships; 33 Scottish Cups; 26 Scottish League Cups; one European Cup Winners' Cup

Club Hero: Davie Cooper – hugely talented winger who played for Rangers for 12 years, helping them to win three league championships and three Scottish Cups. He died in 1995 and the 2005 League Cup final, contested between two of his ex-clubs, Rangers and Motherwell, was named the 'Davie Cooper Final' in tribute to him.

Biggest Win: Rangers 10 – Hibernian 0 (1898)

Biggest Defeat: Airdrieonians 10 – Rangers 2 (1886)

Fan Fact: In 1872, Rangers and Dumbarton finished on equal points at the top of the league and it was decided that there would be a play-off to decide who would be crowned champions. However, the match was tied and so the league title was shared for the only time in Scottish football history.

Best Pub for Away Fans: The Europa

ST JOHNSTONE

Nickname: The Saints

Ground: McDiarmid Park, Perth

Honours: Six Tier Two titles; one Challenge Cup

Club Hero: Sandy Clark – manager who led St Johnstone to third place in the Scottish Premier League, the Scottish League Cup Final, and the Scottish Cup semi final in the 1998–1999 season.

Biggest Win: St Johnstone 13 – Tulloch 0 (1887)

Biggest Defeat: Cowdenbeath 12 – St Johnstone 0 (1928)

Fan Fact: Manchester United manager, Sir Alex Ferguson, scored a hat-trick for St Johnstone in a victory over Rangers in 1963.

Best Pub for Away Fans: The 208 Bar

ST MIRREN

Nickname: The Buddies

Ground: St Mirren Park, Paisley

Honours: Four Tier Two titles; three Scottish Cups

Club Hero: Mark Yardley – imposing striker who played for the club for eight years. He scored less than a minute into his St Mirren debut.

Biggest Win: St Mirren 15 – Glasgow University 0 (1960)
Biggest Defeat: Rangers 9 – St Mirren 0 (1897)
Fan Fact: The club are named after the saint who founded Paisley Abbey and who is the patron saint of the town.
Best Pub for Away Fans: The Cottage Arms

EUROPEAN CLUBS

AC MILAN (ITALY)

Nickname: Rossoneri (the Red-Blacks)
Ground: San Siro, Milan
Honours: 17 League Championships; five Coppa Italia (Italian Cups); seven European Cups; two European Cup Winners' Cups; five European Super Cups; one FIFA Club World Cup
Club Hero: Franco Baresi – cultured defender who played for the club for his entire career, helping them win six league titles and two European Cups. The number 6 shirt at AC Milan has been retired in his honour.
Biggest Win: AC Milan 9 – Palermo 0 (1951)
Biggest Defeat: Ajax 6 – AC Milan 0 (1974)
Fan Fact: AC Milan were founded by a group of five Englishmen. They were led by the lace-maker Herbert Kilpin, who was born in Nottingham and went on to become the club's first captain.

AFC AJAX (NETHERLANDS)

Nickname: Godenzonen (Sons of the Gods)
Ground: Amsterdam Arena, Amsterdam
Honours: 29 League Championships; 18 KNVB Cups (Dutch Cups); four European Cups; one European Cup Winners' Cup; one UEFA Cup; two European Super Cups
Club Hero: Johan Cruyff – phenomenally talented forward who had two spells at Ajax as a player and went on to become the club's manager. He was instrumental in the club's three successive European Cup wins in the early 1970s and also helped pioneer the Total Football style of play. The number 14 shirt has been retired in his honour.

Biggest Win: Ajax 14 – Red Boys Differdange (Luxembourg) 0 (1984)

Biggest Defeat: Feyenoord 9 – Ajax 4 (1964)

Fan Fact: Ajax are one of only three clubs to have won all three major European trophies (the European Cup, the UEFA Cup, and the European Cup Winners' Cup). Juventus and Bayern Munich are the other two clubs that have achieved this feat.

BARCELONA (SPAIN)

Nickname: Barça

Ground: Camp Nou, Barcelona

Honours: 20 League Championships; 25 Copa del Rey (Spanish Cup); three European Cups; four European Cup Winners' Cups; three Fairs Cups; three European Super Cups

Club Hero: Carles Puyol – consistent defender who has only ever played for Barcelona and became club captain in 2004. He helped the club win an unprecedented treble of the Champions League, La Liga (League Championship) title, and Copa del Rey (Spanish Cup) in the 2008–2009 season.

Biggest Win: Barcelona 10 – Tarragona 1 (1949)

Biggest Defeat: Athletic Bilbao 12 – Barcelona 1 (1931)

Fan Fact: Barcelona have been involved in European club competition every year since 1955, and are the only club to hold this record.

BAYERN MUNICH (GERMANY)

Nickname: Die Bayern (The Bavarians)

Ground: Allianz Arena, Munich

Honours: 22 League Championships; 15 DFB-Pokal (German Cup); four European Cups; one European Cup Winners' Cup; one UEFA Cup

Club Hero: Franz Beckenbauer – elegant defender who played for the club for 13 years and went on to become manager. As a player he helped Bayern win the European Cup three years in succession in the mid 1970s.

Biggest Win: Bayern Munich 11 – Borussia Dortmund 1 (1971)

Biggest Defeat: Schalke 7 – Bayern Munich 0 (1976)

Fan Fact: When the Bundesliga (German League) was formed at the start of the 1963–1964 season, Bayern were not admitted because the authorities only wanted to include one team from each city, and 1860 Munich had performed better in the regional league in the previous year.

Half Time Quiz ☉
Which two teams have met most often at World Cup finals?
   (Answer: Brazil and Sweden have met seven times at World Cup finals: they played each other once in 1938, 1950, 1958, 1978 and 1990; and twice in 1994.)

INTERNAZIONALE (ITALY)

Nickname: I Nerazzurri (The Black and Blues)
Ground: San Siro, Milan
Honours: 18 League Championships; six Coppa Italia (Italian Cups); three European Cups; three UEFA Cups
Club Hero: Giacinto Facchetti – innovative defender who spent his entire career at the club; he was a key part of the famous 'Great Inter' team of the early 1960s that won back-to-back European Cups. He went on to become the club's president in 2004. The number 3 shirt was retired in his honour after his death in 2006.
Biggest Win: Inter Milan 16 – Vicenza Calcio 0 (1915)
Biggest Defeat: Juventus 9 – Inter Milan 1 (1961)
Fan Fact: In 1929, the name of the club was changed to AS Ambrosiana by the club's new president Oreste Simonotti. This change proved unpopular with the fans and after the end of the Second World War the name was changed back to a close approximation of the original title.

OLYMPIQUE LYONNAIS (FRANCE)

Nickname: Les Gones (The Kids)
Ground: Stade Gerland, Lyon
Honours: Seven League Championships; four Coupe de France (French Cups); one Coupe de la Ligue (French League Cup)
Club Hero: Sidney Govou – creative forward who has played for the club for his entire career. He was a key part of the Lyon

team that won the league championship seven seasons in a row in the 2000s.

Biggest Win: Lyon 10 – AC Ajaccio 0 (1953)

Biggest Defeat: Inter Milan 7 – Lyon 0 (1958)

Fan Fact: Prior to their triumph in the 2001–2002 season, Lyon had never won the French League Championship. They then went on to win the title a record-breaking seven years in a row.

FC PORTO (PORTUGAL)

Nickname: Dragões (The Dragons)

Ground: Estádio do Dragão, Porto

Honours: 24 League Championships; 15 Taça de Portugal (Portuguese Cups); two European Cups; one UEFA Cup; one European Super Cup

Club Hero: José Mourinho – talented manager who led the club to two Portuguese titles, as well as the UEFA Cup and Champions League titles.

Biggest Win: Porto 15 – SC Sanjoanense 1 (1942)

Biggest Defeat: Benfica 12 – Porto 2 (1943)

Fan Fact: Porto won the UEFA Cup in the 2002–2003 season, then went on to win the Champions League in the 2003–2004 season; this was the first time that a club had won both trophies in succession since Liverpool achieved the same feat in the 1975–1976 and 1976–1977 seasons.

REAL MADRID (SPAIN)

Nickname: Los Blancos (The Whites)

Ground: Estadio Santiago Bernabéu, Madrid

Honours: 31 League Championships; 17 Copa del Rey (Spanish Cups); nine European Cups; two UEFA Cups; one European Super Cup; three FIFA Club World Cups

Club Hero: Alfredo di Stéfano – immensely talented forward who played for the club for 11 years, then went on to have two spells as manager. He was hugely influential in the Madrid team that dominated the European Cup in the 1950s.

Biggest Win: Real Madrid 11 – Elche 2 (1960)

Biggest Defeat: Espanyol 8 – Real Madrid 1 (1930)

Fan Fact: Real Madrid have won both the UEFA Cup and the European Cup, but have never won the European Cup Winners' Cup; they lost the final in 1971 to Chelsea, and in 1983 to Aberdeen.

Half Time Quiz ⚽

Which player has played against Liverpool in both an FA Cup final and a European Cup final?

(Answer: Laurie Cunningham. He played for Wimbledon when they defeated Liverpool in the 1988 FA Cup final, and he played for Real Madrid when they lost the 1981 European Cup final to Liverpool.)

5

THE STORY OF THE STADIUMS: FOOTBALL GROUNDS

Football grounds provoke many emotions: love, loathing, nostalgia and even apathy. Their atmospheres can be as passionate as bubbling cauldrons, or as sterile as hospital waiting rooms. Many are revered like favourite players, while others are despised like hated rivals. But their most surprising feature is that a stadium's story can often be as fascinating as the matches played inside.

👟 IT'S JUST NOT CRICKET: 👟 EARLY FOOTBALL GROUNDS

In the early days of the modern game, it became clear that the public were willing to pay for the privilege of watching their local teams, and enterprising clubs realised that a significant source of income could be derived from charging admission to matches. At first, this meant that football teams had to borrow grounds that were used for other sports: mainly cricket. For example, the first ever international match, played between Scotland and England, took place at the West of Scotland Cricket Ground. Soon purpose-built grounds were springing up all over the United Kingdom, and the captivating story of the football ground began.

OLDEST FOOTBALL GROUNDS

Much debate surrounds the question of which ground can rightfully call itself 'the world's oldest', but the following grounds can all rightfully call themselves early pioneers.

- **Drill Field, Northwich**. Home to Northwich Victoria, it opened in 1875 but was sold in 2002 to help pay the club's debts.

- **Bramall Lane, Sheffield**. Currently home to Sheffield United, but was originally home to Sheffield Wednesday. It was opened as a cricket ground in 1855 and held its first football match in 1862. It was also the venue of the final of the first ever football tournament – the Youdan Cup.

- **Sandygate, Sheffield**. Home to Hallam FC, it was originally a cricket ground (and occasionally is still used for cricket). The first match was played there in 1860.

- **York Road, Maidenhead**. Home to Maidenhead United, it was also originally a cricket ground but switched to football in 1871.

- **Racecourse Ground, Wrexham**. It hosted an international match between Wales and Scotland in 1877 and the Welsh international team still occasionally play there, making it the oldest continually used international football ground.

👢 YOU'RE STANDING ON MY 👢 FOOT: HIGHEST ATTENDANCES AND LARGEST GROUNDS

As the 20th century wore on, the popularity of football increased exponentially and this meant that football grounds had to cope with ever increasing crowds. In Britain, attendances at the most popular matches were huge.

The highest attendances recorded in Britain are:

- 1937 Scotland *v.* England Home International, Hampden Park, Glasgow: 149,415 (record British attendance)

- 1937 Celtic *v.* Aberdeen Scottish Cup Final, Hampden Park, Glasgow: 146,433 (highest attendance at a British club match)

- 1923 Bolton *v.* West Ham FA Cup Final, Wembley Stadium, London: 127,000 (highest attendance in England)

- 1939 Rangers *v.* Celtic First Division Match, Ibrox Stadium, Glasgow: 118,567 (highest attendance at a British league match)

- 1948 Manchester United *v.* Arsenal, First Division Match, Maine Road, Manchester: 83,260 (highest attendance at an English league match). This match was played at Maine Road (formerly the home of Manchester City) because the war-damage at Old Trafford had not been fully repaired.

Pocket Fact 🏆

Wembley Stadium was so overcrowded during the 1923 FA Cup Final that fans spilled onto the pitch. Police officer George Scorey became famous for shepherding the crowd off the pitch whilst riding a white horse, and the match became known as the 'White Horse Final'.

With the introduction of modern safety rules and all-seater stadiums, such attendances are never likely to be repeated in Britain (currently Wembley is the largest stadium in the UK with a maximum capacity of 90,000), but there are still many places throughout the world where vast crowds squeeze into venues to watch their favourite teams.

The largest grounds in the world used primarily for football are:

1. **Yuva Bharati Krirangan** (also known as the Salt Lake Stadium), Kolkata, India. Capacity 120,000. Opened in 1984, the Salt Lake Stadium is home to three teams: Mohun Bagan Athletic Club, East Bengal FC, and Mohammedan Sporting Club, and also often hosts the Indian national team.

2. **Estadio Azteca**, Mexico City, Mexico. Capacity 105,000. Opened in 1966, it is home to the Mexican national team and the club side, Club América. It is also the only stadium to have hosted two World Cup finals (1970 and 1986).

3. **Azadi Stadium**, Tehran, Iran. Capacity 100,000. Opened in 1971, it is home to Persepolis FC and Esteghlal FC as

well as the Iranian national team. 'Azadi' means 'freedom' in Persian.

4. **Camp Nou**, Barcelona, Spain. Capacity 98,787. Home to Barcelona, it was opened in 1957. Camp Nou (which means 'new field' in Catalan) hosted the semi final between Italy and Poland at the 1982 World Cup.

5. **Soccer City**, Johannesburg, South Africa. Capacity 94,700. Opened in 1989, Soccer City is the largest football stadium in Africa. It was the venue for Nelson Mandela's first speech after he was released from prison and also hosted the 2010 World Cup final.

🥾 FOOTBALL'S MOST 🥾
CONTROVERSIAL STADIUMS

Some football grounds are famous for their intimidating atmosphere; famous examples include Galatasaray's Ali Sami Yen Stadium, Paris Saint-Germain's Parc des Princes and Dinamo Zagreb's Stadion Maksimir. At these grounds, the fans make a concerted effort to intimidate opposition teams. However, it is not always the fans that are responsible for making a football ground an unpleasant place to visit. The history of football is sprinkled with examples of teams refusing to play in certain stadiums for reasons that have nothing, or very little, to do with football.

Most objectionable stadiums

- **Estadio Nacional de Chile**, Santiago, Chile. In 1973, the Soviet Union refused to play the second leg of their play-off against Chile for a place at the 1974 World Cup, as the match was to be held at the Estadio Nacional. This was because Chile had recently undergone a military coup, and during the aftermath of this event the military government used the stadium to detain prisoners, some of whom were later executed. FIFA were not impressed with the Soviet's refusal to play the match and disqualified them from the World Cup.

- **Al-Shaab Stadium**, Baghdad, Iraq. The Al-Shaab Stadium (which means 'People's Stadium' in Arabic) is home to the Iraq national team in principle only, as FIFA have prevented the Iraqi national team from playing their home ties in Iraq due to security concerns since the 2003 invasion. However, the Palestinian national team (as recognised by FIFA) have played two friendlies against Iraq in the stadium, with Iraq winning on both occasions.

- **Ramat Gan Stadium**, Ramat Gan, Israel. The Ramat Gan Stadium is home to the Israeli national team, but has not hosted any of Israel's near-neighbours in more than three decades. The Israeli national team was originally a member of the Asian Football Confederation (AFC), even hosting the Asian Nations Cup in 1964. However, after the 1973 Yom Kippur War, relations between Israel and its neighbours collapsed, and almost every nation in the Middle East refused to play in Israel. This ultimately led to Israel's expulsion from the AFC; the country is now a member of UEFA and takes part in European World Cup qualifying and international tournaments.

- **Estadio Hernando Siles**, La Paz, Bolivia. Home of the Bolivian national team, this stadium is situated at 3,637 metres above sea level. At this height, engaging in an endurance sporting activity (such as a 90 minute football match) becomes very difficult if a player has not adapted to the conditions. Most other South American teams have voiced strong complaints with FIFA over the advantage that playing at this altitude gives to the Bolivians.

Pocket Fact 🏆

In May 2007, FIFA banned teams from holding World Cup qualifying matches at more than 2,500 metres above sea level. This meant that Bolivia were no longer allowed to play at the Estadio Hernando Siles. However, after pressure from Bolivian president Evo Morales, FIFA relented and the stadium is back in use.

👞 EVERYBODY NEEDS GOOD 👞 NEIGHBOURS: FOOTBALL'S CLOSEST GROUNDS

In football, great rivalries are most often based on proximity: the closer the fans are to each other, the more likely they are to wind each other up. Due to this, the most passionate club rivalries are often between teams that share the same city. However, some sets of fans not only have to put up with being in the same city as their rivals, but also being on the same street. Here are some grounds within a long goal kick of each other:

- **Dens Park and Tannadice Park, Dundee**. Home to Dundee and Dundee United respectively, these two stadiums are situated on the same street (although fans of both clubs are keen to point out that technically Dens Park is on Sandeman Street and Tannadice is on Tannadice Street) and are the closest football grounds in the United Kingdom.

- **Stadion Hidegkuti Nándor and Sport Utcai Stadion, Budapest, Hungary**. Home to MTK Hungária and BKV Előre respectively, the two stadiums back on to each other. However, the clubs do not play in the same league: MTK Hungária are in the Hungarian Premier League, while BKV Előre play in the second tier.

- **Meadow Lane and The City Ground, Nottingham**. Notts County play their home games at Meadow Lane, while Nottingham Forest play their matches at the City Ground. The two stadiums are less than 300 metres apart, but a journey between them would involve getting a bit wet as they are separated by the River Trent.

- **Goodison Park and Anfield, Liverpool**. Goodison and Anfield are separated by Liverpool's Stanley Park. As Anfield is home to Liverpool, and Goodison is home to Everton, these two teams possibly boast the greatest animosity of all the close neighbours.

Pocket Fact 🏆

While some city rivals have to share the same street, there are others who do not even have to share the same continent. Istanbul's two great footballing rivals, Galatasaray and Fenerbahçe, are situated only a few miles from each other, but due to the unique geographical situation of the city, Galatasaray's stadium is in Europe, while Fenerbahçe's is in Asia.

👟 TERRIBLE GAME, GREAT VIEW: 👟 THE BEAUTIFUL GAME IN BEAUTIFUL SETTINGS

There are some moments when even the most die-hard football fan has to admit that the match they are watching is rubbish: innumerable attacking moves have broken down before they have even started, neither team has managed to string together more than three passes, and the goalkeepers look like they are about to doze off. In the overwhelming majority of football grounds, fans have no choice but to carry on watching the mediocrity unfold; however, in a few rare places, there is another option. Dotted throughout the world are football stadiums where the surrounding landscape or impressive architecture is often much more captivating than the football.

Here are a few grounds where there is an alternative to watching your useless centre forward constantly hoof the ball over the crossbar:

- **Stade Louis II**, Monaco. Home to AS Monaco, the Stade Louis II is a doubly impressive place to watch a match. Not only is it one of football's most architecturally impressive grounds (the nine arches situated behind one of the goals are one of football's most iconic design features), it is also no more than a stone's throw from the Mediterranean in the picturesque principality of Monaco. The Stade Louis II is the venue for the annual European Super Cup final.

- **Svangaskarð**, Toftir, Faroe Islands. Home to B68 Toftir and formerly home to the Faroe Islands national team, Svangaskarð is perched on a windswept rocky hillside overlooking an inlet of the Atlantic Ocean. The Faroe Islands national team do not have a very impressive record, so visiting international fans often got to witness an emphatic victory for their team (unless they happen to be fans of Scotland), as well as one of the best views to be found at a football ground.

- **Pita Stadium**, Pita, Japan. Sometimes referred to as the 'Big Eye' due to the resemblance to an eye when viewed from above, the Pita Stadium is one of football's most unique stadiums. Opened in 2001, it was host to three World Cup matches during 2002 and is home to the J-League side, Pita Trinita. The futuristic outward appearance is matched by its spectacular modern interior.

- **Rheinpark Stadion**, Vaduz, Liechtenstein. Rheinpark Stadion is home to both FC Vaduz and the Liechtenstein national team. As its name suggests, it is very close to the River Rhine (which acts as the Liechtenstein-Swiss border) and also boasts spectacular views of the surrounding mountains of the Alps. Both the English and Welsh national teams have enjoyed successful results (if not impressive performances) in the Rheinpark Stadion in recent years.

- **Allianz Arena**, Munich, Germany. Opened in 2005, the Allianz Arena is home to Munich's two main football teams, Bayern Munich and 1860 Munich, and also occasionally hosts the German national team. The stadium is surrounded by special panels that can be lit up in three different colours: red when Bayern Munich are playing, blue when 1860 Munich are at home, and white when the German national team visit. It is the only ground in the world that can boast this feature. The stadium was host to six World Cup matches in 2006, including the opening game and one of the semi finals.

🥾 STADIUM INNOVATIONS 🥾

Relentless innovation has kept football grounds thoroughly modern; new ideas are constantly being dreamed up and incorporated into stadiums both young and old. Some key features of a modern stadium include:

- **The Press Box**. First introduced at Celtic Park in 1894, the press box is a section of a stadium where journalists are given space to take notes while watching the game.

- **Floodlights**. An essential feature to allow matches to be played at night, the Football League was initially opposed to their use but bowed to the inevitable in the 1955–1956 season. Portsmouth and Newcastle contested the first league match to be floodlit on 22 February 1956.

- **Undersoil Heating**. The British climate often refuses to cooperate with football fixtures and many games are called off due to frozen pitches. To prevent this from happening, teams began introducing undersoil heating; Goodison Park, home of Everton, was the first ground in Britain to install this feature.

🥾 GONE BUT NOT FORGOTTEN: 🥾 FOOTBALL'S LOST STADIUMS

Football is always in a state of flux; styles change, tactics change, players move on, managers are sacked. It is this fact that keeps the game exciting, otherwise after more than a century of the same teams playing each other in an ever-repeating pattern, fans would have grown bored and the game would have died. However, while change can often be exciting – a new manager, a new striker, or a new formation – it can also be hard for football fans, who are more often than not a highly nostalgic bunch, to move on and accept the new order. Probably the best example of the contradictory feelings of enthusiasm and sadness experienced by fans is the emotional rollercoaster of moving to a new stadium. The lure of a shining modern stadium can be intoxicating, but for many fans it is a wrench to leave behind an old ground, and all the memories that were created inside.

Here are three grounds that fans have shed a tear over leaving behind:

- **Highbury**, London. Highbury (or Arsenal Stadium, to give its formal name) was home to Arsenal between 1913 and 2006. The ground was particularly famous for its two art deco stands (parts of which have been incorporated into a new housing development on the site) and small pitch. The Gunners won their last match at Highbury, beating Wigan Athletic 4–2. They have now moved to the Emirates Stadium.

- **Ninian Park**, Cardiff. The former home of Cardiff City, Ninian Park was built in 1910 and demolished in 2009. The ground also often hosted the Welsh national team and was the venue for a rally by Pope John Paul II during his visit to the UK in 1982. Cardiff's last match at Ninian Park was a disappointing affair: they lost 3–0 to Ipswich Town. Cardiff are now based at the Cardiff City Stadium. Ninian Park was demolished in 2009 and the site has also been turned into a housing development.

- **Wembley Stadium**, London. Home of the English national team, Wembley of course still exists, but in an entirely new form. Completed in 1923, and originally called the Empire Stadium, the old stadium with its iconic twin towers was built for the British Empire Exhibition of 1924. It was the home to the FA Cup final for more than 70 years, as well as the venue for England's 1966 World Cup triumph. In 2003 it was knocked down and work began on an entirely new stadium, but the memories of countless footballing heroes climbing the famous 39 steps to collect their medals and trophies will live on.

Pocket Fact 🏆

Between 2001 and 2006, while the new Wembley Stadium was being constructed, the final of the FA Cup was held at the Millennium Stadium in Cardiff.

6

WHO'S IN CONTROL? OWNERSHIP

Modern football teams are no longer owned solely by traditional chairmen, instead many are now controlled by foreigners, their own fans and even by internet companies. This chapter will examine the changing nature of club ownership, detailing the different models and even explaining how anyone can get involved.

🥾 FOOTBALL CLUB STRUCTURE: 🥾 WHO'S WHO OFF THE PITCH

At a football club, there's a holy trinity – the players, the manager and the supporters. Directors don't come into it. They are only there to sign the cheques.
Bill Shankly

Modern football clubs are hugely complex institutions and running them requires a large army of staff. The majority of clubs have the same organisational structure:

Chairmen. The owner of the club, they choose who to employ as manager and often provide the money to fund transfer deals.

Manager. The person who is in charge of making football-related decisions, such as picking the team, choosing what formation to use and what areas to focus on in training. (See Chapter 7 for more on managers.)

Coaches. They work with the players on an individual level, helping them to improve their game. Most teams have different coaches for different areas, such as goalkeeping, defence and attack.

Scouts. They assess the strengths and weaknesses of opponents and also seek out potential new signings.

🥾 CHAIRMEN 🥾

A large number of football clubs operate at a financial loss – the wages and transfer fees that they spend are not covered by the money that they earn. Obviously, this state of affairs is not sustainable; however, in some cases rich chairmen invest their own money in football teams, thus allowing them to carry on spending. Traditional chairmen tended to be local business owners; however, super-rich foreign chairmen are becoming increasingly common in the British game.

THE OLD GUARD

Owning clubs used to the sole preserve of rich local business owners whose motivations were simple: they wanted the team they supported to do well and sought to bask in the glamour and prestige that surrounds football. They often owned business in the local area and had strong links with the clubs they invested in. Successful chairmen who were also fans include:

- **Jack Walker, Blackburn Rovers**. Walker was born and bred in Blackburn and so when he made his fortune, he decided to heavily invest in his hometown club, Blackburn Rovers. Walker took control of the club in 1991, at a time when they were stuck in the second tier of English football, and by the end of the 1994–1995 season they were the champions of England. He passed away in 2000, but a trust he set up continues to help fund the team to this day.

- **Fergus McCann, Celtic**. Although born in Scotland, McCann has Canadian nationality – but no one can doubt his love for Celtic, the club he took over in 1994. McCann led Celtic from near-bankruptcy back to the top of Scottish football during his rather brief five year chairmanship of the club.

Pocket Fact 🏆

UEFA rules stipulate that a person may not have a controlling interest in more than one club that takes part in any UEFA competition.

Chairmen can gain a great deal of popularity among the local fans if they can bring success; however, if the team starts to perform badly, or the fans feel that the chairmen is interfering with the manager's decisions to the detriment of the club, then the supporters often begin to turn against the owners. Chairmen who have suffered the ire of the fans include:

- **Mike Ashley, Newcastle United**. Ashley took control of Newcastle in 2007 and was initially very popular with the fans, due to his unconventional style and because he convinced fan favourite Kevin Keegan to return as manager. The fans began to turn against him though when Keegan resigned, and he became even more unpopular after Newcastle's relegation from the Premier League at the end of the 2008–2009 season.

- **Peter Ridsdale, Leeds United**. Ridsdale was chairman of his local team, Leeds United, between 1997 and 2003. His early relationship with the fans was good as he brought success; the club reached the semi finals of the Champions League in the 2000–2001 season. However, it soon became clear that the success had been built on an unstable foundation of debt, and as a consequence of this, the club was forced to sell a large number of players. Most fans still hold Ridsdale responsible for the subsequent decline that saw the club plunge as low as the third tier.

Pocket Fact 🏆

In 2009, Tranmere Rovers were put up for sale in a rather unique way. The owner, Peter Johnson, had employed an American company to help find a buyer for the struggling club, *and they decided to list the club on the internet trading site eBay with a starting price of $10 million (approx. £6.8 million). Johnson was not impressed and quickly had the listing removed.*

THE NEW BREED

Many of Britain's most famous clubs have recently been taken over by foreign chairmen. These men (football ownership has remained almost completely dominated by men) rarely have any meaningful connection to the clubs that they invest in, and instead view football clubs either as a business investment or a badge of wealth similar to large houses, yachts and expensive cars. However, this lack of local roots does not mean that these new directors have been unsuccessful; in fact many clubs have enjoyed great success under foreign ownership. Prominent foreign chairmen include:

- **Roman Abramovich, Chelsea**. Russian billionaire Abramovich made his money from a wide range of business and became the owner of Chelsea in 2003. His large investment in new players helped the club to win the 2004–2005 English Premier League title, their first league title since the 1954–1955 season. During his time in charge, Chelsea have had six different managers.

- **Vladimir Romanov, Hearts**. Romanov is a Lithuanian who has led an interesting life; he served on a Soviet submarine during the Cold War, before making his fortune in banking and manufacturing after the break-up of the USSR. He became Hearts chairman in 2005 and has had mixed success – during his first full season in charge the club finished second in the League and won the Scottish Cup, but since then results have deteriorated and Romanov has developed a reputation for interfering with team selections.

While some foreign chairmen have been able to deliver the beginning of (or a return to) a golden age for the team they have invested in, others have been much less successful. Some fans have been angered by the fact that their clubs have been taken over by people whom they perceive to have little respect for the history of their team, while others feel that their clubs are being taken advantage of by unscrupulous business owners whose only interest is profit. Chairmen who have failed to win over the fans include:

- **Malcolm Glazer, Manchester United**. The American billionaire Malcolm Glazer took full control of Manchester United in 2005. The club have enjoyed a great deal of success during Glazer's ownership, winning three successive league titles and their third Champions League trophy. However, many fans were angered by the fact that Glazer incurred huge debts in the take-over, and secured them against the club's assets. This frustration led to some fans setting up a new club, FC United of Manchester, and to many fans wearing green and yellow scarves (the colours of Newton Heath, the original name of Manchester United) to signal their anger over Glazer's ownership of the club.

- **George Gillett and Tom Hicks, Liverpool**. Gillett and Hicks, both Americans, assumed control of Liverpool in 2007 and promised to build a new stadium in Stanley Park, close to Anfield. Gillett and Hicks' relationship with the fans began to deteriorate when the new stadium failed to materialise and it became clear that there were problems developing between the two owners and the club's manager, Rafael Benitez. In April 2010, Gillett and Hicks announced that they had put Liverpool up for sale.

FOOTBALL'S MOST CONTROVERSIAL CHAIRMEN

Some chairmen bring money and new players to a club; others bring the police and the tabloid press. Here are some chairmen who have given their club the wrong kind of publicity:

- **Stan Flashman, Barnet**. Flashman presided over a successful period in Barnet's history, but will always be best known for his penchant for sacking managers; he sacked former Barnet manager Barry Fry on eight separate occasions.

- **Jim McLean, Dundee United**. Jim McLean won Dundee United's only League title while he was the club's manager in the 1980s; however, he will possibly be best remembered for his outspoken style while chairman of the club, a position he held until 2000. He retired after assaulting the BBC journalist John Barnes during a post match interview.

- **Ken Richardson, Doncaster Rovers**. Ken Richardson does not have a wonderful record as a football team owner: in fact, most Doncaster fans can reel off a long list of his calamitous decisions. However, his master-stroke was paying an ex-SAS soldier to burn down the club's Belle Vue Stadium. Unfortunately for Richardson, the police found out and he was sent to prison for four years.

FAN OWNERSHIP

Some clubs are more democracy than dictatorship; instead of being controlled by a director, they are run by their own fans. This type of ownership is more common in other European countries, but there are a few examples in the United Kingdom.

GERMANY

The fan truly is king in German football: by law at least 51% of each German football club must be owned by their supporters, and this prevents any rich investor from gaining a controlling interest in a club. This has had many positive benefits for German football: ticket prices have been kept relatively low; most clubs have maintained stable business models and not run up large debts; and teams have kept a connection with their local communities. However, it has been argued that the ban on out-side investment in German football has meant that top German club sides have failed to keep pace with top teams from Spain and England.

SPAIN

Spain's two largest football teams, Real Madrid and Barcelona, in a sense have it both ways: they are controlled by their fans, but also have presidents. Each club has around 100,000 members who each have to pay an annual membership fee, and every four years the members vote for a club president. This democratic approach prevents anyone who is unpopular with the fans from gaining any control over either club, but has not prevented rich patrons from investing heavily in players and infrastructure, thus allowing Barcelona and Real Madrid to enjoy the best of both worlds.

Pocket Fact 🏆

Some of history's most notorious figures have controlled football clubs. During the Soviet era the Russian team, Dynamo Moscow, was strongly associated with the Soviet security services. This led to the infamous head of the Soviet secret police, Lavrentiy Beria, becoming president of the club.

UNITED KINGDOM

Fan-owned clubs are rare in the UK and the majority of teams continue to be owned and controlled by rich directors. The few examples that do exist have usually come about due to extraordinary circumstances: unpopular radical change at the club or significant financial difficulties have forced the fans to step in to take control themselves. Clubs where the fans now call the shots include:

- **Exeter City**. The fans took over Exeter City in 2003, after massive debts coupled with relegation out of the Football League threatened the team's continued existence. Fortunately, fundraising and a hugely profitable FA Cup run during the 2004–2005 season helped the club to regain financial stability, and the balance-sheet success was repeated on the pitch when the club regained its Football League status in 2008.

- **AFC Wimbledon**. AFC Wimbledon was founded in 2002 by former fans of Wimbledon FC who had been greatly angered by the decision to uproot the club and move it to Milton Keynes. The new team is controlled by a supporters' trust that promises to maintain ownership of at least 75% of the club's shares. AFC Wimbledon has enjoyed a meteoric rise through the leagues since its inception: they have achieved four promotions and currently play in the Conference National.

Ebbsfleet United and www.myfootballclub.co.uk

In 2007, the former football writer Will Brooks decided he wanted to buy a football club. Unfortunately he lacked the resources, but fortunately he had an ingenious plan: to create a website that charged its members a small fee in order to amass enough money to purchase a football team. Members would be allowed to vote on matters as diverse as player transfers and kit design. The plan captured the imagination of the public and the website attracted enough members to be able to bid to take over a team, and so in 2008, www.myfootballclub.co.uk took control of the Conference National team, Ebbsfleet United. The club went on to lift the FA Trophy at Wembley Stadium a few months after the takeover.

The website continues to operate and there are plans to start up similar schemes in various other countries throughout the world.

7

LEGENDS: FAMOUS PLAYERS AND MANAGERS

The most famous players and managers are not always the most talented; some are controversial, some are inspirational, some are record breakers, and some are quite simply incompetent. But they all share one common feature: they are all uniquely interesting.

👟 PLAYERS 👟

Players become famous for a huge variety of reasons: leadership, passion, ridiculous haircuts, law-breaking, and even occasionally for their footballing abilities. Football's most fascinating characters are revealed below.

CROWD PLEASERS: FOOTBALL'S SHOWMEN

Football is a team game and every player within the team is equally important. However, not every player is equally exciting; some players light up matches with their mesmerising skills. Here are some of the most exciting players ever to kick a ball:

George Best

Nationality: Northern Irish

Clubs: Manchester United (1963–1974); Cork Celtic (1975–1976); Los Angeles Aztecs (1977–1978); Fulham (1976–1978); Hibernian (1979–1981); San Jose Earthquakes (1980–1981)

Honours: European Footballer of the Year 1968

Best is probably the most skilful footballer that the United Kingdom has produced. He was famous for both his other-worldly talent and the celebrity lifestyle he adopted, which curtailed his football career and tragically shortened his life. He famously stated: 'I spent a lot of money on booze, birds and fast cars. The rest I just squandered'. But perhaps a more fitting tribute to the player is a saying common among his greatest fans: 'Maradona good; Pelé better; George Best'.

Half Time Quiz ☉

Who is the only winner of the European Footballer of the Year title to have played a league match for a Scottish team?

(Answer: George Best, who played for Hibernian. Denis Law, the only Scottish player to win the accolade, never played for a Scottish club side.)

Johan Cruyff

Nationality: Dutch

Clubs: Ajax (1964–1973 and 1981–1983); Barcelona (1973–1978); Los Angeles Aztecs (1979–1980); Washington Diplomats (1980–1981); Feyenoord (1983–1984)

Honours: European Footballer of the Year 1971, 1973 and 1974; 1974 World Cup Golden Ball

Cruyff is the greatest player never to have won the World Cup. He was part of the famous Ajax and Holland teams that utilised the 'Total Football' philosophy of play, winning the European Cup three times in a row with Ajax and reaching the World Cup final with the Dutch national team. He is one of the rare breed of footballers who have enjoyed great success as a player and as a manager – he won four league titles and two European trophies as Barcelona manager in the late 1980s and early 1990s.

Eusébio

Nationality: Portuguese

Clubs: Sporting Clube de Lourenço Marques (1957–1960); Benfica (1960–1975); Toronto Metros-Croatia (1976); Las Vegas Quicksilvers (1977)

Honours: European Footballer of the Year 1965; 1966 World Cup Golden Boot

Eusébio began his career in Mozambique, the country of his birth, and was originally going to sign for Sporting Lisbon before the move was hijacked by the Benfica manager Béla Guttmann. Eusébio, or the Black Pearl as he was popularly known, went on to become Benfica and Portugal's greatest ever player. His awesome dribbling ability helped Portugal finish third at the 1966 World Cup, and was central to Benfica's victory over Real Madrid in the 1962 European Cup final.

Lionel Messi

Nationality: Argentinian

Clubs: Barcelona (2004–present)

Honours: European Footballer of the Year 2009; FIFA World Player of the Year 2009

Messi moved to Barcelona at an early age, and while the switch from South America to Europe has damaged the career of many young players, it has proved to be a great decision for the player, his club, and all fans of football. His diminutive size (he is 5 foot 7 inches) has not prevented him from becoming modern football's shining light. The devastating combination of incisive passing, intricate dribbling, and lethal finishing propelled Barcelona to the historic treble of the Spanish League title, Spanish Cup and Champions League in the 2008–2009 season.

Pocket Fact 🏆

Lionel Messi was sent off less than two minutes into his full international debut; he was substituted on in a friendly match between Argentina and Hungary and was sent off almost immediately for elbowing an opponent.

I ALSO PLAY FOOTBALL: FOOTBALLERS FAMOUS OFF THE PITCH

The world-wide popularity of football has meant that many famous players have used the recognition they gained from playing the game to launch themselves in other careers. Here are some players who have turned on-field fame into off-field success:

David Beckham

Nationality: English

Clubs: Manchester United (1993–2003); Real Madrid (2003–2007); LA Galaxy (2007–present); AC Milan (2009 & 2010)

Honours: FIFA World Player of the Year Runner-up 1999 and 2001

David Beckham has possibly become more famous for being a cultural icon than a football player. He frequently takes part in fashion shoots, has his own perfume, endorses countless products, and is married to former Spice Girl, Victoria. However, Beckham's activities outside of football should not distract from the fact that he remains one of England's most talented players – at his peak he was the most deadly free-kick taker in the world and he captained his country at two World Cup finals.

Pocket Fact 🏆

Some football players have become famous for playing more than one sport. The Russian forward Vsevolod Bobrov, who played football for both the Soviet Union and CSKA Moscow, went on to win a gold medal at the Winter Olympics as part of the Soviet Union ice hockey team.

George Weah

Nationality: Liberian

Clubs: Tonnerre Yaoundé (1987–1988); AS Monaco (1988–1992); Paris Saint-Germain (1992–1995); AC Milan

(1995–2000); Chelsea (2000); Manchester City (2000); Olympique Marseille (2000–2001); Al-Jazira (2001–2003)

Honours: European Footballer of the Year 1995; FIFA World Player of the Year 1995

George Weah is one of Africa's greatest ever players and remains the only African to have won European Footballer of the Year. He spent the majority of his career playing in Europe, but returned to Liberia after his retirement to run for political office. In 2005 he was one of the front-runners to become president of Liberia, but lost to Ellen Johnson Sirleaf in the final ballot. He served as a UN Goodwill Ambassador and has been actively involved in charity work in his home country.

Gary Lineker

Nationality: English

Clubs: Leicester City (1978–1985); Everton (1985–1986); Barcelona (1986–1989); Tottenham Hotspur (1989–1992); Nagoya Grampus Eight (1992–1994)

Honours: 1986 World Cup Golden Boot

Gary Lineker was one of the greatest forwards that England has ever produced; he sits second on the list of all-time goal scorers for the English national team (he scored one goal less in his career than Bobby Charlton), and remains the only English player to have won the Golden Boot at the World Cup finals. And he has continued to enjoy a high media profile since his retirement from the game: he became the anchorman of the BBC's football programme, *Match of the Day*, in 1999; he was one of the team captains on the sports comedy programme, *They Think It's All Over*; and has become the advertising face of a famous brand of crisps.

Pocket Fact 🏆

Gary Lineker holds a perfect disciplinary record: he was never yellow or red-carded during his entire career.

Michel Platini

Nationality: French

Clubs: Nancy (1972–1979); AS Saint-Étienne (1979–1982); Juventus (1982–1987)

Honours: European Player of the Year 1983, 1984 and 1985

Michel Platini is France's most celebrated player; blessed with Gallic flair and fierce determination, he helped Juventus win the European Cup in 1985 and France win the European Championships in 1984. In recent years however, he has become more famous for his role as UEFA president. Elected to the post in 2007, Platini has been a controversial head of European football – he has called for caps on wages, limits on the number of foreign players that clubs can field and has been critical of large transfer fees. These bold policy directions have meant that his fame as a footballer may one day be eclipsed by his fame as an administrator.

Great Nicknames

Football has a strong tradition of giving players nicknames; it is a way to celebrate the great and mock the not-so-great. Some nicknames are clever, some are meaningful and some are simply hilarious. Here are five of the best:

- *Il Divin Codino (The Divine Ponytail): Roberto Baggio. The Italian international was famous for both his silly hairstyle and his exceptional footballing talent, and so earned a nickname that combined the two.*
- *El Buitre (The Vulture): Emilio Butragueño. The Spanish international famously played for Real Madrid during the 1980s and 1990s, earning his nickname for his lethal ability in front of goal.*
- *The Incredible Sulk: Nicolas Anelka. Anelka has played for a vast number of clubs, including Arsenal, Real Madrid, Liverpool, Manchester City and Fenerbahçe, but whichever team he plays for, he never seems to smile.*

> • *Rombo di Tuono (Sound of Thunder): Luigi Riva.*
> *Riva played for the Italian national team in the 1960s and*
> *1970s and remains Italy's all-time record goal scorer. His*
> *nickname derives from the fact that he had an extremely*
> *powerful shot.*

BACKBONE OF THE TEAM: INSPIRATIONAL PLAYERS

Great teams need great players, but the greatest teams need players who possess both talent and presence. Here are some players who have made the greatest teams tick:

Franco Baresi

Nationality: Italian

Clubs: AC Milan (1977–1997)

AC Milan were the best club side in the world in the period between the late 1980s and the early 1990s. Their success was built on a foundation of defensive stability, and the beating heart of the AC Milan defence was Franco Baresi. Baresi's superb organisational ability gave those players beside him in defence both confidence and reassurance, and those in front of him free-rein to attack the opposition. With Baresi as the defensive anchor, AC Milan were able to go on a 58 match unbeaten run in the Italian league between 1991 and 1993. AC Milan retired his number 6 shirt as a tribute to the role he played at the club.

Ferenc Puskás

Nationality: Hungarian

Clubs: Kispest (1943–1949); Budapest Honvéd (1949–1955); Real Madrid (1958–1966)

The Hungarian national team were unstoppable in the early and mid 1950s; they defeated England 6–3 at Wembley, the first time the English had lost at home to continental opposition, and only lost one match in the period between 1950 and 1956. During this time, the Hungarian team overflowed with talented players, but the central figure and captain was Puskás. His mercurial genius and unique footballing intelligence bound the team together and made them better than the sum of their parts. But Puskás did more than just create, as his scoring record for Hungary is beyond impressive: he scored 84 goals in 85 games. Political problems forced Puskás to leave Hungary in 1958, but he is still revered as the country's greatest player – as demonstrated by the fact that Hungary's national stadium is named after him.

Pocket Fact 🏆

Puskás played at World Cup finals with two different teams; he played at the 1954 World Cup for Hungary, and then after electing to play for the Spanish national team, played for Spain at the 1962 World Cup.

Franz Beckenbauer

Nationality: German

Clubs: Bayern Munich (1964–1977); New York Cosmos (1977–1980 & 1983); Hamburg (1980–1982)

Honours: European Player of the Year 1972 and 1976

Sometimes, the exceptional talent of one player allows a team to adopt a unique tactical style. This was particularly true of the West German national team in the 1970s: Franz Beckenbauer was in theory deployed as a sweeper, but in practice he was the axis around which the rest of the team turned. He marshalled the West German defence when the opposition were in possession, and dictated the form each attack would take when they regained the ball. Simply put, he was a manager's dream: a world-class defender who was composed and creative with the ball at his feet.

Pocket Fact 🏆

Franz Beckenbauer is the only player to have both captained and managed a World Cup winning team. He achieved this feat as West Germany captain in 1974 and manager of Germany in 1990.

Pelé

Nationality: Brazilian

Clubs: Santos (1956–1974); New York Cosmos (1975–1977)

Honours: 1970 World Cup Golden Ball; FIFA Player of the Century

So much hyperbole surrounds the world's greatest ever footballer that it has become difficult to put his talent in perspective. However, one simple fact illustrates the influence he exerted in the game: when Pelé made his debut for Brazil in 1957, the Brazilians had never won the World Cup; by the time he retired from international football in 1971 they had lifted the trophy three times. Pelé was by no means a one-man team, and in fact played a limited role in Brazil's 1962 World Cup victory, but it was his brilliance that demonstrated once and for all to the world, and more importantly to the Brazilian people, that the Samba style of football that the Brazilians practiced could be successful as well as attractive to watch. This realisation was Pelé's greatest gift to Brazil and to football.

Half Time Quiz ☻

Name the players who have scored in more than one World Cup final.
    (Answer: Only four players have achieved this feat: Vavá (1958 and 1962) and Pelé (1958 and 1970) for Brazil; Paul Breitner (1974 and 1982) for West Germany; and Zidane (1998 and 2006) for France.)

HERO OR VILLAIN? CONTROVERSIAL PLAYERS

There are some highly talented players who are as famous for their bad behaviour as their footballing ability. Here are some players who have crossed the line into infamy:

Eric Cantona

Nationality: French

Clubs: Auxerre (1983–1988); Marseille (1988–1991); Nimes (1991); Leeds United (1992); Manchester United (1992–1997)

So much talent was squeezed into Eric Cantona's body that there obviously was not any room for modesty and self-control. Cantona, with his iconic up-turned collar and confident stare, was one of the key players in Manchester United's explosive revival under Alex Ferguson, but he was also very quick to anger. His major indiscretions include spitting at a Leeds United fan upon his return to Elland Road with Manchester United, repeatedly fighting with teammates throughout his career, and, most famously, kicking a Crystal Palace fan after being sent off in January 1995. Since retiring from football he has developed a cult following as an actor, appearing in several films including *Looking for Eric*.

Pocket Fact 🏆

Eric Cantona is the only player to have won England's top division in consecutive seasons with different clubs: he won the 1991–1992 title with Leeds United and went on to win the 1992–1993 title with Manchester United.

Paul Gascoigne

Nationality: English

Clubs: Newcastle United (1985–1988); Tottenham Hotspur (1988–1992); Lazio (1992–1995); Rangers (1995–1998);

Middlesbrough (1998–2000); Everton (2000–2002); Burnley (2002); Gansu Tianma (2003); Boston United (2004)

Paul Gascoigne never failed to provoke a reaction: throughout his entire career fans were either in awe of his incredible technical ability, or overwhelmed by his unbelievable stupidity. He remains a legend at almost every team he played with for good reason: a last minute goal for Lazio in the Lazio-Roma derby; a hat-trick for Rangers against Aberdeen to win the league title; a wonderful free kick for Tottenham to take them to the FA Cup final and count-less iconic moments for the England national team. But there were also the moments that verged on the moronic: two severe injuries as the result of rash tackles; repeated bouts of binge drinking; and pretending to play a flute at an Old Firm derby in order to anger Celtic fans.

Zinedine Zidane

Nationality: French

Clubs: Cannes (1988–1992); Bordeaux (1992–1996); Juventus (1996–2001); Real Madrid (2001–2006)

Honours: European Player of the Year 1998; FIFA World Player of the Year 1998, 2000 and 2003; 2006 World Cup Golden Ball

Zidane was one of the most talented footballers of his generation and during his long career he won all of football's major honours – the World Cup, the Champions League, and Italian and Spanish league titles. However, it was not only his masterful talent that made him famous; Zidane was also renowned for having a very short temper. The most famous example of this was during the 2006 World Cup final when Zidane was sent off for headbutting the Italian defender Marco Materrazi during extra time. A documentary film was made about Zidane: it involved 17 cameras tracking his movements during a Spanish league match. This film encapsulates Zidane's career; he displays breath-taking brilliance when in possession of the football, but then gets sent off in the dying minutes for his involvement in a mass brawl.

Half Time Quiz ⚽

Who was the first player to be sent off in a World Cup final?

(Answer: Pedro Monzon for Argentina in 1990. Four other players have been sent off in World Cup finals: Gustavo Dezotti, also for Argentina in 1990; Marcel Desailly for France in 1998; and Zinedine Zidane, also for France in 2006 and Johnny Heitinga for the Netherlands in 2010.)

Diego Armando Maradona

Nationality: Argentinian

Clubs: Argentinos Juniors (1976–1981); Boca Juniors (1981–1982 and 1995–1997); Barcelona (1982–1984); Napoli (1984–1991); Sevilla (1992–1993); Newell's Old Boys (1993–1994)

Honours: 1986 World Cup Golden Ball

Some players' careers can be summed up in just one or two moments. For Maradona, those two moments happened in the same match: the 1986 World Cup quarter final between Argentina and England. Early in the second half, he blatantly and deliberately used his hand to divert the ball into the goal in what became known as the 'Hand of God' incident. This was cheating at its worst. However, four minutes later, Maradona produced an example of football at its best: starting from inside his own half, Maradona beat four English players, rounded the goalkeeper and stroked the ball into the net. The Argentines won the match and went on to lift the World Cup. His football skills made him a saint, but his behaviour – twice banned from football for failing drugs tests, tax evasion whilst playing in Italy – made him a sinner. Maradona was appointed coach of Argentina in 2008 and has remained a controversial figure: he was banned from any involvement in football for two months by FIFA after repeatedly swearing at the press during a media conference.

Youth versus Experience

Football is an intensely physical sport; it requires strength, speed, stamina and agility, and this means that most professional footballers fall into the age range of around 18–34. However, there are some impressive exceptions. Here are some of football's youngest and oldest record breakers:

- **Oldest player to score at a World Cup finals**. Roger Milla (42 years and 39 days) for Cameroon against Russia at the 1994 World Cup.
- **Youngest player to score at a World Cup finals**. Pelé (17 years 239 days) for Brazil against Wales at the 1958 World Cup.
- **Youngest player to appear at a World Cup finals**. Norman Whiteside (17 years 41 days) for Northern Ireland against Yugoslavia at the 1982 World Cup.
- **Youngest player to appear in the Football League**. Reuben Noble-Lazarus (15 years 45 days) for Barnsley against Ipswich Town in the Championship in 2008.
- **Oldest player to score in the Premier League**. Teddy Sheringham (40 years 268 days) for West Ham United against Portsmouth in 2006.

Half Time Quiz ☉

Which player has scored for five different teams in the Champions League/European Cup?

(Answer: Hernan Crespo. He has scored in the competition for AC Milan, Chelsea, Internazionale, Lazio and Parma.)

SAFE HANDS: GREATEST GOALKEEPERS

Goalkeepers have the oddest role in football: they spend most of the game standing around doing nothing; become the most important player on the field for a few moments; and then shout angrily at their defenders for a couple of minutes. Mastery over these three areas requires character, concentration, agility, and strength. Here are some of the world's greatest goalkeepers:

Dino Zoff

Nationality: Italian

Clubs: Udinese (1961–1963); Mantova (1963–1967); Napoli (1967–1972); Juventus (1972–1983)

Dino Zoff is the holder of many impressive records: he was only the second goalkeeper to captain a World Cup-winning side; he did not concede a goal in an international match for an impressive 1,142 minutes (more than 12 games) between 1972 and 1974; and he won the European Championships in only his fourth appearance for the Italian national team. However, Zoff's career was not simply about records: he was also a hugely impressive goalkeeper known for his intimidating presence, his committed work ethic, and his perfectionism. After he retired from playing, Zoff went on to become a successful manager, winning the UEFA Cup with Juventus and reaching the final of the European Championships with Italy.

Pocket Fact 🏆

Dino Zoff is the oldest player to have won the World Cup; when Italy triumphed in the 1982 final against West Germany, Zoff was 40 years old.

Gordon Banks

Nationality: English

Clubs: Chesterfield (1955–1959); Leicester City (1959–1967); Stoke City (1967–1972); Cleveland Stokers (1967); Fort Lauderdale Strikers (1977–1978)

Gordon Banks will forever be remembered by England fans for two great moments: helping England win the 1966 World Cup, and his save from a Pelé header in the first round of the 1970 World Cup. For all his incredible talent, Banks did not win a large number of trophies in his long career; apart from the 1966 World Cup, he only lifted two League Cups – one with Leicester City and the other with Stoke City. However, in football, ability is often more important than accolades, and what Banks lacked in the latter, he more than made up for in the former.

Sepp Maier

Nationality: German

Clubs: Bayern Munich (1962–1979)

Sepp Maier won every honour football has to offer: four German League titles; three European Cups; the 1972 European Championship; and the 1974 World Cup. But his greatest achievement may be that he was able to stand out in a German national team which included world-class players such as Franz Beckenbauer and Gerd Müller. Maier was nicknamed 'The Cat' because of his super-human agility and was well known for his enthusiastic sense of humour. He was also an impressively consistent player; he did not miss a league match for Bayern Munich between 1966 and 1977.

Lev Yashin

Nationality: Russian

Clubs: Dynamo Moscow (1949–1971)

Honours: European Footballer of the Year 1963

The European Footballer of the Year award has been running for 54 years, and in that time it has only been won once by a goalkeeper, Lev Yashin. Yashin, whose nickname was the 'Black Spider', is widely recognised as being the greatest goalkeeper in the history of the game. He won the European Championship with the USSR in 1960, and helped Dynamo Moscow win five Soviet league championships. He was famous for organising his defence (by shouting orders at them) and for his tendency to race out of his penalty area to intercept opposition through-balls, but he will always be best remembered for his extraordinary goalkeeping talent.

Pocket Fact 🏆

Since 1994, the prize for the best goalkeeper at the World Cup finals has been known as the 'Lev Yashin Award'. Past winners include Fabian Barthez, Oliver Kahn and Gianluigi Buffon.

👟 MANAGERS 👟

Managers are usually the first to be blamed when a team performs poorly, and among the last to be praised when the team enjoys success. Their careers are filled with frustration, worry, and criticism from both fans and the press. So who would want to be a manager? Below are some of the most famous people to take on football's most stressful job.

WE'LL NEED A BIGGER TROPHY CABINET: SUCCESSFUL MANAGERS

The most famous managers are often the ones who have enjoyed the greatest success. Below are some of the managers who have led their respective teams into a golden age:

Sir Alex Ferguson

Nationality: Scottish

Teams Managed: East Stirlingshire (1974); St Mirren (1974–1978); Aberdeen (1978–1986); Scotland (1985–1986); Manchester United (1986–present)

Great managers either continually produce success at big clubs, or manage to hugely surpass expectations at smaller clubs; Alex Ferguson has achieved both. In his early career he won three Scottish championship titles and the European Cup Winners' Cup with Aberdeen (after defeating Real Madrid 2–1 in the final). Then came his big move to Manchester United. After a slow start, he finally won the league in the 1992–1993 season, and after that, the floodgates opened and Ferguson turned Manchester United into the most successful club in England. His most impressive triumphs have been twice winning a hat-trick of league titles (1998–1999, 1999–2000,

2000–2001 and 2006–2007, 2007–2008, 2008–2009), and two
Champions League titles (1998–1999 and 2007–2008).

Pocket Fact 🏆

*Alex Ferguson has been Manchester United manager since
November 1986. During this time, Arsenal have had four
different managers, Liverpool six, Chelsea 12, Tottenham also
12, and Newcastle United 14.*

José Mourinho

Nationality: Portuguese

Teams Managed: Benfica (2000); UD Leiria (2001–2002); Porto
(2002–2004); Chelsea (2004–2007); Inter Milan (2008–2010);
Real Madrid (2010–present)

Mourinho enjoyed a greatly advantageous managerial apprentice-
ship, working with both Bobby Robson (initially as his interpreter)
and Louis van Gaal, and this, along with his fierce determination and
assured confidence in his own ability, has enabled him to develop
into one of modern football's greatest managers. Mourinho has
enjoyed spectacular success at every club he has managed: he led
Inter Milan and Chelsea to domestic success (Chelsea's league triumph in 2004–2005 was their first in 50 years), but undoubtedly
his most impressive achievement was Porto's Champions League
triumph in 2003–2004. He has become famous for his arrogance:
he once told an English press conference that he was 'a special one',
but with achievements like his, few can blame him for this vice.

Pocket Fact 🏆

*José Mourinho's teams have not lost a home league match since
February 2002. At the end of the 2009–2010 season,
Mourinho had gone 136 home league matches without defeat –
this included 38 with Porto, 60 with Chelsea and 38 with
Internazionale.*

Arrigo Sacchi

Nationality: Italian

Teams Managed: Rimini Calcio (1984–1985); Parma (1985–1987 and 2001); AC Milan (1987–1991 and 1996–1997); Italy (1991–1996); Atlético Madrid (1998–1999)

Arrigo Sacchi is one of football's more interesting characters. Unlike most managers, he never played football professionally; instead he spent time in various jobs, including a shoe salesman. However, once he began managing, it soon became clear that he possessed a great footballing brain and after a spell at Parma he became manager of one of the world's most famous clubs, AC Milan. While undoubtedly fortunate in the wealth of playing talent at his disposal (his team included Franco Baresi, Frank Rijkaard, Marco Van Basten and Ruud Gullit), Sacchi developed an innovative system to get the best out of all his players. This allowed AC Milan to dominate Italian and European football, winning back-to-back European Cups in 1988–1989 and 1989–1990. After AC Milan, Sacchi went on to manage the Italian national team, leading them to the 1994 World Cup final where they lost on penalties to Brazil.

Bill Shankly

Nationality: Scottish

Teams Managed: Carlisle United (1949–1951); Grimsby Town (1951–1954); Workington (1954–1955); Huddersfield Town (1956–1959); Liverpool (1959–1974)

Bill Shankly had a famous phrase: 'If you are first you are first; if you are second, you are nothing.' This concept summed up Shankly's impact on Liverpool; he turned them from a struggling Second Division side into one of Europe's premier football teams by infusing everyone connected with the club – players, staff, and supporters – with a winning mentality that lingered on at Liverpool long after he retired. He brought great success to the club, but he is also remembered for his relationship with the fans; Shankly believed that the fans were an integral part of a football club and he treated the Liverpool fans with a warmth, dignity, and respect rarely seen in football. Bob Paisley, who was Shankly's assistant and took over as Liverpool manager when he retired, went on to win more trophies than Shankly, but Shankly will always be remembered as Liverpool's, and maybe even Britain's, greatest manager.

Pocket Fact 🏆

Bob Shankly, who was Bill Shankly's brother, was manager of Dundee and took them to the semi finals of the European Cup in 1962–1963.

I WISH I'D THOUGHT OF THAT: GREAT INNOVATORS

Some managers achieve greatness through success, but there are others who have been immortalised because of the importance of their ideas. Below are some managers who have revolutionised the way football is played:

Valeriy Lobanovskyi

Nationality: Ukrainian

Teams Managed: FC Dnipro (1969–1973); Dynamo Kyiv (1973–1982, 1984–1990 and 1997–2002); USSR (1975–1976, 1983–1984 and 1986–1990); United Arab Emirates (1990–1993); Kuwait (1994–1996), Ukraine (2000–2001)

As well as being a gifted footballer, Lobanovskyi was also a highly intelligent scientist, and the Soviet Union of his youth was a country obsessed with the ideal of scientific progress. It was the combination of these factors that led Lobanovskyi to apply scientific techniques to the development of football tactics. He created lists of tasks that each player should perform during a game and adapted these for each match. He also stressed the importance of training and brought in specialists to devise individual training schedules for each of his players. Lobanovskyi was original in that he believed in an analytical style of management, rather than the man-to-man motivational style that many other coaches adopted. And his ideas were successful: he won 13 league titles and two European Cup Winners' Cups with Dynamo Kyiv, and reached the final of the 1988 European Championships with the USSR.

Pocket Fact 🏆

Valeriy Lobanovskyi became the first manager from the Soviet Union to win a European trophy when he lifted the 1985 Cup Winners' Cup with Dynamo Kyiv.

Brian Clough
Nationality: English

Teams Managed: Hartlepool United (1965–1967); Derby County (1967–1973); Brighton and Hove Albion (1973–1974); Leeds United (1974); Nottingham Forest (1975–1993)

Brian Clough's managerial style can best be summed up by one of his most famous quotes: 'Players lose you games, not tactics. There's so much crap talked about tactics by people who barely know how to win at dominoes.' Clough was the antithesis to the ideas of Valeriy Lobanovskyi: he believed that football matches were not won by intricate planning and hours of complex preparation, but instead by motivating players to make them want to play well and win for him and for their club. Clough infused his teams with confidence and self-belief, lavishing them with praise when they played well and subjecting them to the full force of his legendary temper when he believed they had not performed to the best of their abilities. These ideas may have gone out of fashion in the modern game, but they brought Clough great success: he led both Derby County and Nottingham Forest to their first ever English league titles and became only the second English manager to retain the European Cup.

Pocket Fact 🏆

Since 2007, the winner of any match — either in the League, a cup, or as a friendly — played between Derby County and Nottingham Forest will receive the Brian Clough Trophy.

Rinus Michels

Nationality: Dutch

Teams Managed: Ajax (1965–1971 and 1975–1976); Barcelona (1971–1975 and 1976–1978); Netherlands (1974, 1984–1985, 1986–1988 and 1990–1992); Los Angeles Aztecs (1979–1980); FC Köln (1980–1984); Bayer Leverkusen (1988–1989)

Rinus Michels won an enviable number of trophies in his career, including the European Cup (with Ajax) and the European Championships (with Holland), but he will be remembered for one thing above all else: the introduction of the game's most exciting tactical system, Total Football. Michels realised that the creative flair of his best attacking players, in particular Johan Cruyff, was being stifled by opposition defensive tactics, and so he devised an ingenious solution to overcome this problem – he simply set his players free. In his new style of play there would be no rigid positional system; instead each player would become an attacker or defender depending on where he was needed most. It was football's greatest idea since the invention of passing, and the only sour note was that Michels' Dutch team lost in the 1974 World Cup final.

Gustav Sebes

Nationality: Hungarian

Teams Managed: Budafoki MTE (1945–1946); Hungary (1949–1957)

While Gustav Sebes is not very famous, the same cannot be said for his ideas. As manager of the all-conquering Hungary team in the early to mid 1950s, Sebes created a new position that continues to form the core of many of today's best teams – the playmaker.

Up to that point, almost every team had played with three strikers, and these three players were normally marked by three opposition defenders. Sebes decided to withdraw one player from the forward line and move him into a position between the midfielders and the forwards. This player was to be the team's creative outlet, dictating the pace and direction of their attacks. This simple positional shift caused huge problems for opposition defences – if a defender moved out of position to mark the playmaker, it left a space at the back, but if they chose not to mark him, then he was given unlimited time on the ball. This defensive quandary continues to cause problems to this day. While it would be misleading to suggest that Sebes' tactical innovation was entirely responsible for Hungary's dominance – they won a record 32 consecutive matches in the early 1950s – it is almost impossible to overestimate the historical importance of his ideas.

Short Managerial Careers

Some managers are given time to build an empire at their club; others are not given enough time to boil the kettle. Here are five managers whose reigns were shorter than a goldfish's attention span:

- **Brian Clough**. *44 days at Leeds United in 1974. Not the shortest managerial reign by any means, but Clough's brief term at Leeds is one of the most famous due to David Peace's book,* The Damned United. *Clough was sacked due to poor results (he only won one out of seven games) and a difficult relationship with the Leeds squad.*

- **Micky Adams**. *13 days at Swansea City in 1997. Adams claimed he was promised significant transfer funds to improve the team. However, this money did not materialise and Adams left after only three games, all of which ended in Swansea defeats.*

- **Kevin Cullis**. *Seven days at Swansea City in 1996. Cullis was a PE teacher who lacked any professional managerial experience, but the incoming Swansea chairman, Michael*

Thompson, decided he would be ideal for the job of Swansea manager. He wasn't. After two defeats, Cullis resigned and Thompson's takeover was called off.

- **Dave Bassett**. Four days at Crystal Palace in 1984. Bassett was offered the Crystal Palace job whilst he was manager of Wimbledon and he accepted. After four days he decided he had made a mistake and returned to Wimbledon.

- **Leroy Rosenior**. 10 minutes at Torquay United in 2007. Undoubtedly the shortest managerial reign of all time, Rosenior was appointed Torquay manager by the club's owner, Mike Bateson. However, within 10 minutes of Rosenior officially accepting the job, Bateson had sold his controlling share in Torquay to new owners who decided they wanted to appoint their own manager, so Rosenior was sacked.

Half Time Quiz ☻

Which manager has managed the greatest number of different teams at the World Cup finals?

(Answer: Bora Milutinović has coached five different teams at the World Cup: Mexico (1986), Costa Rica (1990), USA (1994), Nigeria (1998), and China (2002).)

8

WINNING IS EVERYTHING: CUPS AND COMPETITIONS

The life of a football fan is filled with many painful emotions: energy-sapping tension, utter disgust, and often crushing disappointment. However, these pale into insignificance when compared to the euphoria that comes with winning a trophy. From small-scale domestic leagues, to the grandest of all competitions, the World Cup, football has a vast array of leagues, cups and competitions that bring heartache and ecstasy to fans year after year.

👟 FOOTBALL COMPETITIONS: 👟 LEAGUES, CUPS, AND TOURNAMENTS

Football teams take part in a variety of competitions, but the most common types all follow a similar format. The main types of football competition are:

Leagues

Leagues involve a set number of teams playing each other both home and away over the course of a season. Most commonly, three points are awarded for a win and one point for a draw. In the majority of leagues, if two teams finish the season with the same number of points, they are separated by goal difference (the number of goals they scored minus the number of goals they conceded). Major football leagues rarely have less than 10 or more than 24 participants.

Cups

In cup competitions, teams are drawn into pairs, who then play each other with the winner advancing to the next round. In some cup competitions, such as the FA Cup, each tie only involves one match, but in others, such as the latter stages of the Europa League, each tie is played over two legs with each team playing one match at home and one match away. The winner is the team with the better aggregate score. Ties are played until there are only two teams left; these two teams then contest the cup final, which almost invariably involves one match at a neutral venue.

Tournaments

Tournaments usually involve a mixture of the league format and the knockout cup format. The most famous tournament in football is the World Cup, which involves teams being drawn into groups who all play each other in a round robin format, with the highest placed teams advancing to the next round. The latter rounds involve teams playing each other in single knockout matches, with the winner advancing to the next round and the loser being eliminated. The Champions League follows a roughly similar format to the World Cup.

👟 DOMESTIC CUPS 👟

In the United Kingdom the cups came before the leagues, and this was reflected in the respect they were accorded by both clubs and fans. Today, almost all fans view cup competitions as an important chance for their club to lift some silverware.

FA CUP (ENGLAND)

The FA Cup, which began in the 1871–1872 season, is football's oldest cup competition. It was started by the Football Association to encourage the public to take an interest in the new sport of football, and has gone on to become one of the game's most prestigious competitions.

Eligible Teams

The teams eligible for the FA Cup are all teams from the Premier League, the Football League and the first four levels of the FA National League system. Additionally, teams from the fifth and sixth levels of the National League system whose grounds meet the entry requirements are granted places. In the 2009–2010 season, this amounted to 762 teams.

Did you know:

- Wanderers, a team from the Battersea area of London captained by the FA Cup's founder CW Alcock, won the first two FA Cups, and triumphed in the tournament a further three times during the 1870s, but the team was disbanded before the beginning of the 20th century.

- A Scottish team, Queen's Park, reached the FA Cup final twice (1884 and 1885) but lost both times to Blackburn Rovers.

- Early FA Cups were also won by a university team (Oxford University in 1874) and a team representing an army corps (Royal Engineers in 1875).

- None of the teams that were triumphant in the first 10 FA Cup finals would go on to lift the trophy in the 20th century.

- Manchester United have won the FA Cup 11 times; the biggest number of wins in the history of the competition.

One of the most celebrated aspects of the FA Cup is the continual shocks that the tournament throws up.

Famous FA Cup shocks:

- Sunderland's 1–0 victory over Leeds United in the 1973 final. Leeds were the holders and were contesting the Cup Winners' Cup final 11 days later (while Sunderland had finished sixth in the Second Division), but an Ian Porterfield goal sent the cup home with Sunderland.

- Barnsley managed two great shocks in the same year during the 2007–2008 competition; they defeated Liverpool at Anfield in the fifth round, then won 1–0 against Chelsea at their own Oakwell ground in the quarter final. They lost to Cardiff in the semi final.

- Hereford, a non-league side, defeated Newcastle, who were in England's top division, 2–1 in the third round of the

1971–1972 competition. Hereford had forced a replay after drawing 2–2 at St James' Park.

Half Time Quiz ☉

Who was the first player to be sent off in an FA Cup final?
(Answer: Manchester United's Kevin Moran received a red card in the 1985 final against Everton. Manchester United won the match 1–0.)

SCOTTISH CUP (SCOTLAND)

Impressed by the success of the FA Cup, the Scottish Football Association decided to create its own cup competition, and so the Scottish Cup came into existence in the 1873–1874 season.

Eligible Teams

Teams from the Scottish Premier League and the three divisions of the Scottish Football League; in addition, teams playing in the Highland Football League, the South of Scotland League, the East of Scotland League, and four teams from the Scottish Junior Football Association are allowed entry to the Scottish Cup. A total of 81 teams entered the Scottish Cup in the 2009–2010 season.

Pocket Fact ♛

Celtic hold the title of most Scottish Cup wins, with 34 wins to their name.

The Scottish Cup has provided many great shocks, but two of the most famous are:

● Inverness Caledonian Thistle's 3–1 win over Celtic at Celtic Park in the third round in 2000. Celtic were suffering a drop in form under new manager John Barnes, but this was the lowest point for both club and manager. Barnes was sacked soon after the game.

- Berwick Rangers' 1–0 win over Rangers in 1967. An inspired performance by future Rangers manager Jock Wallace in the Berwick goal helped his team to secure their greatest ever victory.

Pocket Fact 🏆

The original Scottish Cup trophy, first used in the inaugural 1873–1874 competition, is still in use. This makes it the oldest surviving national football trophy in the world.

👞 DOMESTIC LEAGUES 👞

Almost every country in the world has its own football league and the creation of a national league is often among the first acts of newly independent nations. In most countries, the league title is the most prestigious domestic prize.

BUNDESLIGA (GERMANY)

The Bundesliga is the youngest of Europe's major football leagues, having only been established in 1963.

- **Number of teams**: 18

- **Relegation**: The bottom two teams are relegated, and the third bottom team takes part in a two-leg play-off against the third placed team in the Bundesliga.

- **Most titles**: Bayern Munich – 21.

Half Time Quiz ⚽

Which is the only team to have taken part in every season of the Bundesliga?

(Answer: Hamburg, who were part of the inaugural Bundesliga and have never been relegated.)

J. LEAGUE DIVISION 1 (JAPAN)

Professional football in Japan only began in 1993 with the introduction of the J. League. Since that time, the Japanese league has grown to become the strongest league in Asia.

● **Number of teams**: 18

● **Relegation**: The bottom three teams are relegated to the J. League Division 2 and replaced by the top three teams from the J. League Division 2.

● **Most titles**: Kashima Antlers – 7.

Pocket Fact 🏆

Former England international Gary Lineker ended his career playing in the J. League for Nagoya Grampus Eight.

MAJOR LEAGUE SOCCER (USA)

There have been many attempts to establish a professional football league in the United States, but the MLS, which has been running since 1993, seems to have succeeded where others have failed.

● **Number of teams**: 16

● **Relegation**: Due to the complex nature of sports franchising in the United States, there is no relegation from the MLS.

● **Most titles**: DC United – 4.

Pocket Fact 🏆

In 2004, Freddy Adu became the youngest player in MLS history, when he came on as a substitute for DC United at the age of 14.

PREMIER LEAGUE (ENGLAND)

The Premier League, formerly known as the First Division, is the longest running football league in the world, having begun in the 1888–1889 season.

- **Number of Teams**: 20

- **Relegation**: The bottom three teams are relegated to the Championship. The top two teams in the Championship gain promotion, along with the winner of a play-off between the four teams that finished third to sixth.

- **Most titles**: Manchester United and Liverpool – 18.

Pocket Fact 🏆

Only two teams have managed to remain undefeated for an entire season in the top division in England: Preston North End in the 1888–1889 season and Arsenal in the 2003–2004 season.

PRIMERA DIVISIÓN (SPAIN)

Commonly referred to as La Liga, the Primera División was founded in 1929 and the first winners were Barcelona.

- **Number of teams**: 20

- **Relegation**: The bottom three teams are relegated to the Segunda División. The top two teams in the Segunda Division gain promotion along with the winner of a play-off between the four teams that finished third to sixth.

- **Most titles**: Real Madrid – 31.

Pocket Fact 🏆

Only nine different teams – Real Madrid, Barcelona, Atlético Madrid, Athletic Bilbao, Valencia, Real Sociedad, Deportivo, Sevilla, and Real Betis – have won the league title in Spain.

SERIE A (ITALY)

Serie A was founded in 1929, although a league competition had existed in various forms in Italy as far back as the 19th century.

- **Number of teams**: 20

- **Relegation**: The bottom three teams are relegated to Serie B. The top two teams from Serie B are promoted, along with the team that finished third providing they finished 10 or more points clear of the fourth placed team. If the gap between third and fourth is less than 10 points, the teams that finished third to sixth play-off for the final promotion place.

- **Most titles**: Juventus – 27.

League Dominance

The changing nature of football means that success is often hard to sustain over long periods. However, there have been impressive examples of teams exerting a monopoly on league success.

- ***Skonto FC****. Won 14 Latvian titles between 1991 and 2004. The Latvian League (known as the Virsliga) was formed in 1991 after the break-up of the Soviet Union. Skonto FC, who are from the Latvian capital Riga, went on to win the first 14 league championships. This impressive run of success remains a world record.*

- ***Rosenborg BK****. Won 13 Norwegian titles between 1992 and 2004. Rosenborg's dominance of the Norwegian League, the Tippeligaen, was an example of a virtuous circle of success. Victory in the league allowed them to qualify for the Champions League (a feat they achieved eight times in a row between 1995 and 2002), and the resources this provided helped to ensure continued league success.*

- ***Celtic****. Won nine Scottish titles between 1966 and 1974. Celtic won the league nine seasons in a row under legendary manager Jock Stein. During this period Celtic also won the European Cup, becoming the first British club to do so.*

> • *Rangers*. Won nine Scottish titles between 1989 and
> 1997. *The first three league successes were masterminded by
> manager Graeme Souness; however, he left the club in 1991
> and was replaced by Walter Smith, who guided the club to
> their ninth title in a row in the 1996–1997 season, thus
> equalling Celtic's record.*

👟 CURRENT EUROPEAN 👟
COMPETITIONS

Domestic success can bring glory to a club, but it is only in the
crucible of European competition that true champions are
revealed. Victory in a European club competition proves to the
footballing world that a club deserves to be remembered.

CHAMPIONS LEAGUE

The Champions League, known as the European Cup until the
1992–1993 season, is the premier European club competition.
The first competition took place during 1955–1956 and the
winners of the inaugural tournament were Real Madrid, who
went on to win the first five titles.

- **Qualification**: Originally, only the champions of the domestic
  leagues of the various members of UEFA were eligible to play
  in the tournament. However, the rules were altered in the
  1997–1998 season to allow the second placed teams in the
  larger leagues to gain entry. Further changes continue to be made
  and the current competition allows up to four entrants from each
  individual nation, depending on the strength of the league. A
  total of 76 teams from 52 countries entered the 2009–2010
  tournament, with 32 qualifying for the initial group stage.

- **Most wins**: Real Madrid – nine (1956, 1957, 1958, 1959,
  1960, 1966, 1998, 2000 and 2002).

- **Impressive Records**:

  - 17 different German teams have taken part in the
    competition.

- AC Milan, Ajax, Barcelona, Internazionale, Liverpool, Manchester United, Marseilles, and Red Star Belgrade, have all won the trophy without losing a game.

- Real Madrid's Spanish forward, Raúl, is the leading scorer in the competition with 66 goals.

Half Time Quiz ☻

Who is the only player to have won the Champions League with three different clubs?

(Answer: Clarence Seedorf. He won the trophy with Ajax in 1995, Real Madrid in 1998, and AC Milan in both 2003 and 2007.)

British Milestones in Europe

British clubs have enjoyed many triumphs in Europe. Major milestones on the path of success include:

- **First British team to reach a European final**: *Rangers – 1961 Cup Winners' Cup. Rangers lost 4–1 to Fiorentina over two legs.*
- **First British team to win a European trophy**: *Tottenham – 1963 European Cup Winners' Cup. Tottenham defeated Atlético Madrid 5–1 in the final.*
- **First British team to win the European Cup**: *Celtic – 1967. Celtic defeated Internazionale 2–1 in the final.*
- **First all-British European final**: *Tottenham versus Wolverhampton Wanderers – 1972 UEFA Cup. Tottenham won 3–2 over two legs.*

EUROPEAN SUPER CUP

The Super Cup began in 1972, and is an annual one-off match played at the start of each season. Traditionally it was contested by the winners of the Champions League and the European

Cup Winners' Cup. However, since the demise of the Cup Winners' Cup at the end of the 1998–1999 season, the winners of the Europa League have taken part instead. Between 1972 and 1997 the match was played over two legs; in 1998 this was replaced with a one-off match held at the Stade Louis II in Monaco.

- **Qualification**: The European Super Cup is contested by the winners of the Champions League and the Europa League.

- **Most wins**: AC Milan – five (1989, 1990, 1994, 2003 and 2007)

Half Time Quiz ⚽

Who are the only three managers to have won the European Cup/Champions League with two different clubs?

(Answer: Ernst Happel (Feyenoord 1970 and Hamburg 1983); Ottmar Hitzfeld (Borussia Dortmund 1997 and Bayern Munich 2001); and José Mourinho (Porto 2004 and Internazionale 2010).)

EUROPA LEAGUE

The Europa League, formerly known as the UEFA Cup, is UEFA's second most important European tournament. A new format, that saw the introduction of a round-robin group stage involving 12 groups of four teams, was introduced at the start of the 2009–2010 season. After the initial group stage, the competition reverts to a straight knock-out format. Atlético Madrid became the first winners of the Europa League after beating Fulham 2–1 in the 2010 final.

Qualification

The tournament accepts entrants based on league standing, success in domestic cup competitions, and three additional places are granted to teams from the leagues with the highest UEFA Fair Play ranking. Furthermore, teams that are knocked out of the Champions League in the third qualifying round, or the play-off round and the teams who finish third in the Champions League group stage, drop into the Europa League.

⚽ PAST EUROPEAN COMPETITIONS ⚽

UEFA CUP

The UEFA Cup was created in 1971 as a replacement for the Fairs Cup, and became one of the most important European club competitions. The tournament saw a large number of format changes between its introduction in 1971 and its replacement by the Europa League at the end of the 2008–2009 season. These changes included the altering of the final from a two-legged tie to a one-off match for the start of the 1997–1998 season, and the increase in the number of entrants in 1999 after the demise of the Cup Winners' Cup.

- **Qualification**: Initially, qualification for the UEFA Cup was granted to teams who finished in the runners up places in their domestic leagues, but after the demise of the European Cup Winners' Cup, the winners of domestic cup competitions were also allowed entry.

- **Most wins**: Internazionale, Juventus and Liverpool – three titles each.

- **Impressive Records**:

  - All four participants – Eintracht Frankfurt, Bayern Munich, Borussia Mönchengladbach and Stuttgart – in the 1979–1980 UEFA Cup semi finals were from West Germany. Eintracht Frankfurt went on to lift the trophy.

  - Espanyol were undefeated in the 2006–2007 UEFA Cup, recording 11 wins and three draws. However, they did not win the tournament: Sevilla defeated them on penalties in the final after the match ended 2–2.

  - French teams reached the final on four occasions (Marseille in 1999 and 2004; Bordeaux in 1996 and Bastia in 1978), but never once lifted the trophy.

Pocket Fact 🏆

British teams appeared in five of the last 10 UEFA Cup finals, but only Liverpool managed to lift the trophy. Arsenal, Celtic, Middlesbrough and Rangers all fell at the final hurdle.

EUROPEAN CUP WINNERS' CUP

The Cup Winners' Cup was introduced in the 1960–1961 season for the winners of domestic cup competitions, and it ran until the 1998–1999 season. The competition was a two-legged knockout tournament with a one-off final held at a neutral venue. British clubs enjoyed a large degree of success in the Cup Winners' Cup; British teams appeared in 17 of the 39 finals and won the competition on 10 occasions.

- **Qualification**: As its name suggests, teams qualified for the Cup Winners' Cup by winning their domestic cup competition (such as the FA Cup in England or the Scottish Cup in Scotland).

- **Most wins**: Barcelona – four (1979, 1982, 1989 and 1997)

- **Impressive records and controversial moments**:

  - FC Magdeburg became the only team from East Germany to win a major European trophy when they won the Cup Winners' Cup in 1974.

  - Rangers were banned from defending the trophy after their fans invaded the pitch during their 1972 triumph.

  - Bobby Moore won three finals in three years at Wembley; he won the 1964 FA Cup and 1965 Cup Winners' Cup with West Ham, and then the 1966 World Cup with England.

Pocket Fact 🏆

No team managed to retain the European Cup Winners' Cup, although Real Madrid and Sevilla both managed to retain the

> *UEFA Cup, and seven teams have managed to retain the Champions League.*

INTER-CITIES FAIRS CUP

The Inter-Cities Fairs Cup was created in 1955 to help promote trade fairs, and was unique among European competitions in that it allowed cities to enter unified teams made up of players from a series of different clubs. The inaugural competition took three seasons to complete due to organisational difficulties and scheduling conflicts. In 1971, UEFA took over the running of the competition and it evolved into the UEFA Cup.

- **Qualification**: Initially, only teams from cities that held trade fairs were allowed to enter the competition, but after 1968 qualification was granted to teams who finished in the runners up places in their national leagues.

- **Most wins**: Barcelona – three (1958, 1960 and 1966)

- **Fairs Cup trivia**:

  - The London team that entered the inaugural competition was made up of players from 11 different London-based teams.

  - Early competitions limited each city to one entrant, but this rule was relaxed in the 1961–1962 season.

  - Barcelona were allowed to keep the original trophy after winning a play-off match against Leeds United. Barcelona were the first team to win the competition, while Leeds United were the last.

Pocket Fact ♔

The Fairs Cup is the last major trophy that Newcastle United have won; they lifted the trophy in 1969 and have failed to win a major trophy since.

🦗 INTERNATIONAL COMPETITIONS 🦗

Football fans cannot choose the international team they support: some have the good fortune to have been born in Brazil and get to support a team that has won a total of five World Cups; while others have the misfortune to have been born in San Marino and have to support a team that's won fewer than five individual matches in their entire history. However, no matter what team they support, international fans often prove to be the most vocal and passionate followers of the game.

WORLD CUP

Since its relatively humble beginnings in Uruguay in 1930 when just 13 teams entered, the World Cup has grown to become football's most important event. The tournament is held every four years (excepting the 1942 and 1946 competitions, which were cancelled due to the Second World War) and the 2010 event attracted 204 entrants.

- **Qualification**: Teams qualify for the World Cup by taking part in qualification tournaments organised by their continental association (such as UEFA or CONMEBOL). These qualifying tournaments usually involve nations being divided into groups, which then play each other home and away with the teams finishing highest gaining qualification. A total of 32 teams qualified for the 2010 World Cup: this included 13 teams from UEFA (Europe); three from CONCACAF (North and Central America); six from CAF (Africa); five from CONMEBOL (South America); four from AFC (Asia); and one from OFC (Oceania).

- **Most wins**: Brazil – five (1958, 1962, 1970, 1994 and 2002)

- **Impressive Records**:

  - The Brazilian Mario Zagallo was the first person to win the World Cup as both a player and a manager: he won the competition as a player in 1958 and 1962, and went on to win it as a manager in 1970.

- In 1954 West Germany won their first World Cup after defeating Hungary 3–2 in the final, in a match dubbed 'the Miracle of Berne'; they had lost 8–3 to the Hungarians in the group stage.

- Prior to the 2002 World Cup final, Germany and Brazil had never played each other at the tournament.

Pocket Fact 🏆

When German international players meet for a reunion, Uli Stielike is forced to sit in the corner by himself; he is the only German player to miss a penalty in a World Cup penalty shoot-out. He blotted the copybook during the 1982 semi final against France. His teammates saved his blushes by winning the shoot-out 5–4.

EUROPEAN CHAMPIONSHIP

Europe's international football tournament has been running since 1960 and has produced nine different winners (the World Cup has only been won by eight different teams). The tournament is held every four years in the even years between World Cup tournaments.

- **Qualification**: Initially only four teams qualified for the finals; this was expanded to eight in 1984 and to 16 in 1996, and will increase to 24 for the 2016 tournament. To decide qualification, nations are divided into groups who then play each other on a home and away basis. The teams finishing top qualify for the final tournament.

- **Most wins**: Germany – three (twice as West Germany) (1972, 1980, 1996)

- **Impressive Records**:

  - Six players have appeared in four tournaments: Alessandro Del Piero (Italy), Lothar Matthäus (Germany), Peter Schmeichel (Denmark); Lilian Thuram (France), Edwin van der Sar (Netherlands) and Aron Winter (Netherlands).

- Germany holds the record for most appearances at the finals, with 10.

- The Soviet Union appeared in three out of the first four finals, although they only succeeded in lifting the trophy once (in 1960).

Pocket Fact 🏆

Denmark won the tournament in 1992 even though they failed to qualify for the finals — they replaced Yugoslavia, who had withdrawn from the competition due to the outbreak of the Yugoslav Civil War.

AFRICAN CUP OF NATIONS

The African Cup of Nations is unique among major international tournaments in that it is played every two years. The tournament began in 1957, and has recently been the source of controversy because it takes place in January and February, which coincides with the middle of most European domestic leagues. FIFA has pressured the Confederation of African Football to move the tournament to the summer months but they have so far resisted these calls.

- **Qualification**: A total of 16 teams qualified for the 2010 African Cup of Nations, after participating in a group stage which involved nations playing each other home and away in a league format. When the competition is being staged in the same year as a World Cup (such as in 2010), only one qualifying competition is used for both events.

- **Most wins**: Egypt — seven (1957, 1959, 1986, 1998, 2006, 2008 and 2010)

International Football Rivalries

Passion and pride are at the heart of all football matches, and when these are combined with nationalist feeling and historical tensions, emotions tend to run high. Football's most passionate international rivalries include:

- **England and Scotland.** The oldest international rivals in football have a history stretching back into the 19th century. Scotland fans famously ran amok at Wembley Stadium, ripping up the pitch and tearing down goalposts, after Scotland recorded a 2–1 victory in 1977.

- **Germany and the Netherlands.** Germany and the Netherlands have contested some of the most captivating and hardest fought matches in football's history, including the 1974 World Cup final (which West Germany won 2–1), and the 1988 European Championship semi final (which the Netherlands won 2–1).

- **Honduras and El Salvador.** Violent football matches often take on the appearance of wars, but two matches between Honduras and El Salvador in the qualifying stages for the 1970 World Cup took the metaphor one stage too far, when the encounter directly contributed to the outbreak of hostilities. Riots that followed the games greatly increased already heightened tensions, and soon after the two nations fought a short war that resulted in thousands of deaths.

- **Argentina and Brazil.** South America's two strongest teams have enjoyed a torrid history since their first match in 1914. Claims of bribery and poisoning, in addition to foul-tempered encounters, have repeatedly threatened to overshadow the beautiful football that both teams can produce.

COPA AMÉRICA (SOUTH AMERICA)

The Copa América is one of the oldest major international tournaments, having begun in 1916. Originally the competition took place every two years, but starting in 2007 this was altered to every four years.

- **Qualification**: All 10 teams of the CONMEBOL (South American Football Federation) take part and two additional teams are invited to attend. Past invitees include Mexico, Japan, the USA and Costa Rica. All 10 of the CONMEBOL members plus the USA and Mexico took part in the 2007 tournament.

- **Most wins**: Argentina and Uruguay – both 14

GOLD CUP (NORTH AND CENTRAL AMERICA)

The Gold Cup has only been running since 1991, although an earlier continental tournament did exist between 1963 and 1989. The USA has either hosted or co-hosted all 10 editions of the tournament.

- **Qualification**: The three North American teams (USA, Mexico and Canada) automatically qualify, along with five teams from the Central American zone and four from the Caribbean zone.

- **Most Wins**: Mexico – five (1993, 1996, 1998, 2003 and 2009)

Football at the Olympics

Men's football has been part of the Olympics since 1900, and women's football became an Olympic sport in 1996. The success of football at early Olympic events was one of the factors that led to the creation of the World Cup. The format of the competition has caused much controversy, due to the professional nature of football going against the original amateur ethos of the Olympic movement. However, compromise was established in 1992 by only allowing three players over the age of 23 in each squad. Argentina have won the last two men's competitions, while the USA have enjoyed the same success in the women's competition.

9

STRUGGLE AND TRIUMPH: WOMEN'S FOOTBALL

Women's football has overcome significant opposition to become one of today's fastest-growing sports. The professionalism on display in both matches and organisational structure is constantly improving, and this trend looks set to continue.

🥾 BEGINNINGS 🥾

The women's game experienced its first shoots of popularity in countries that came late to football, in particular China and the USA. Traditional football playing nations took much longer to update the 19th-century attitudes that surrounded women playing football; whereas in China and the USA, both genders began playing the game at the same time and this prevented any stigma from being attached to women footballers.

IT'S A MAN'S GAME: BANS ON WOMEN PLAYING FOOTBALL

Some countries were so against women taking up the game that they introduced bans to prevent them from playing:

- The English Football Association banned women from using official pitches in 1921. The ban was not overturned until 1971.

- Women were banned by law from playing football in Brazil until 1975.

- In 1978, the High Court in England upheld a ban on a 12-year-old girl playing football in a boys' team.

By the 1980s women's football was beginning to take root in Europe, with Germany and the Scandinavian countries leading the way, and soon semi-professional leagues and international competitions were being set up.

👟 CLUB COMPETITIONS 👟

Women's club football lacks the resources of the men's game, but professionalism continues to spread throughout the game, which continues to improve the quality of matches and increase the number of supporters. Some women's clubs have formed as offshoots of men's teams, but many others are entirely new entities.

EUROPEAN LEAGUES

The major European women's leagues are:

- **Frauen Bundesliga (Germany)**. The Bundesliga was formed by a merger of the Northern and Southern German women's leagues in 1997. There are 12 teams in the top division. FFC Frankfurt have won the title a record seven times.

- **Damallsvenskan (Sweden)**. A total of 12 teams make up the Damallsvenskan, which is generally viewed as Europe's premier women's league. It began in 1973, making it one of the longest running women's leagues in the world. Umeå IK are the most successful team, having won the league title on seven occasions.

- **FA Women's Premier League (England)**. The Women's Premier League is made up of 12 teams and has been running since 1992. Arsenal Ladies are the most successful team by a considerable distance: they have won the league in 11 of the 16 seasons.

Pocket Fact 🏆

UEFA created a European-wide club competition known as the UEFA Women's Champions League in 2001. Past winners include FFC Frankfurt (three titles), Umeå IK (two titles) and Arsenal Ladies (one title).

UNITED STATES LEAGUES

The world's first fully-professional women's league was set up in the USA in 2000. The Women's United Soccer Association, as it was known, ran into financial difficulties after three seasons and was forced to fold in 2003. However, professional women's football was revived in 2009 with the newly formed Women's Professional Soccer League. This league is made up of eight teams from across America and has been able to attract some of the most famous names in the women's game, such as Marta Viera da Silva and England's Kelly Smith.

 **INTERNATIONAL COMPETITIONS**

Women's international competitions lack the history of their male counterparts, but this has not prevented them from being both popular and successful. Both women's and men's competitions share similar formats.

WOMEN'S WORLD CUP

The World Cup is the pinnacle of any player's career, either male or female. The women's competition began in 1991.

- **1991** Hosts: China; Champions: USA

- **1995** Hosts: Sweden; Champions: Norway

- **1999** Hosts: USA; Champions: USA

- **2003** Hosts: USA; Champions: Germany

- **2007** Hosts: China; Champions: Germany

Pocket Fact 🏆

The 1999 Women's World Cup final between the USA and China held at the Rose Bowl in California, USA, had an attendance of 90,185. This remains the largest ever crowd for a women's sporting event. The USA won the match 5–4 on penalties.

WOMEN'S EUROPEAN CHAMPIONSHIP

The Women's European Championship also began in 1991, although three unofficial tournaments had taken place in the 1980s.

- **1991** Hosts: Denmark; Champions: Germany

- **1993** Hosts: Italy; Champions: Norway

- **1995** Hosts: Germany; Champions: Germany

- **1997** Hosts: Norway & Sweden; Champions: Germany

- **2001** Hosts: Germany; Champions: Germany

- **2005** Hosts: England; Champions: Germany

- **2009** Hosts: Finland; Champions: Germany

Pocket Fact 🏆

The German women's team have played in nine major international finals (six European Championship finals and three World Cup finals) and have lost only once. Norway defeated them 2–0 in the 1995 World Cup final.

👟 FAMOUS PLAYERS 👟

Even though it has only enjoyed a relatively brief history, the women's game has produced a large number of hugely successful and talented stars. Some of the best known players are revealed below:

- **Mia Hamm (USA)**. Probably the most famous female footballer of all time, Hamm became a World Cup winner at the age of 19 when the USA won the 1991 competition, and went on to lift the trophy a second time in 1999. She was named FIFA World Player of the Year in 2001 and 2002. Now retired, she has also written a book about her experiences as a successful player.

- **Brigit Prinz (Germany)**. Europe's greatest ever female player, Prinz has won the World Cup twice and the European Championships five times. She also won the FIFA World Player of the Year three times in a row between 2003 and 2005.

- **Marta Viera da Silva (Brazil)**. Marta, as she is popularly known, is one of the best players in the modern women's game. She surpassed Brigit Prinz's record by winning the FIFA World Player of the Year for a fourth consecutive year in 2009. Marta was the top scorer at the 2007 World Cup and currently plays in the Women's Professional Soccer League in the USA.

- **Kelly Smith (England)**. Kelly Smith is one of England's most consistent performers; she made her debut for the national team against Italy in 1995 and has represented her country at three European Championships and one World Cup. She scored in the 2009 European Championship final in England's 6–2 defeat to Germany. In 2008, Smith was appointed MBE in the Queen's Birthday Honours.

Pocket Fact 🏆

The Italian Serie A club Perugia tried to sign Brigit Prinz and Sweden's Hanna Ljunberg for their men's team, but both women turned them down.

INTERNATIONAL RECORD HOLDERS

Some players have managed to set highly impressive records in the short history of the women's international game.

- **Most international goals**: 158 – Mia Hamm (USA)

- **Most international appearances**: 342 – Kristine Lilly (USA)

- **Most goals at a single World Cup finals**: 10 (at 1991 World Cup) – Michelle Akers (USA)

- **Most World Cup goals**: 14 – Brigit Prinz (Germany)

THE HEART AND SOUL OF THE GAME: FOOTBALL FANS

Football fans are the heart and soul of football – they provide the money, the atmosphere and the enthusiasm. Players and managers may be responsible for results, but fans are responsible for the humanity in football: the humour, the anger and the emotion.

FOLLOWING A TEAM

Supporting a particular club can be the result of genetics – parents passing on the love of a club to their children; geography – many fans simply support the team that is closest to where they live; because of the way a team plays – many fans follow teams like Brazil or Barcelona due to their fast attacking style; or for any number of other reasons. Here are some of the basics of being a football fan:

GOING TO MATCHES

The most important thing a fan can do is to watch their team play. Football grounds range from the small, intimate stadiums of lower-league teams, to the huge, intimidating stadiums of top-level clubs. Smaller clubs often still allow fans to pay at the gate, but matches at larger stadiums are almost entirely all-ticket in the interests of safety and security. Fans that follow their team throughout the season often purchase season tickets: this allows them to save money (the price of a season ticket is smaller than the total price of individual tickets for each match), and to guarantee that they will be able to attend every match.

Pocket Fact 🏆

Season tickets can be an expensive purchase for football fans: during the 2009–2010 season, season tickets in the English Premier League ranged from £250 to £1,850.

DRESSING FOR THE OCCASION

In the modern game, showing support for a team no longer simply involves cheering for them on a Saturday afternoon. Today's committed fans can also own replica shirts, scarves, hats, polo shirts, tracksuits, ties, and many other items emblazoned with their club's colours.

Pocket Fact 🏆

Liverpudlian sailors in the Chilean city of Viña del Mar set up a football team in 1909, and named it after the team they supported in Liverpool, Everton FC – thus creating the team Everton de Viña del Mar. They continue to play in the Chilean Primera División to this day.

LEARNING THE WORDS

When a fan decides to follow a particular team, there are two things they must quickly learn: the words to any team songs and the names of the players and clubs that their team hates. Football fans enjoy nothing more than celebrating their own team's success and insulting their rivals, and this is what generates the vast majority of the noise at any football match.

One big sing-a-long: Football songs

Football fans are not known for their tunefulness, but they usually more than make up for this with their enthusiasm. Many football teams have their own songs that they play before

*the players enter the pitch to get the crowd going. Famous
examples include:*

- You'll Never Walk Alone — *Liverpool and Celtic*
- I'm Forever Blowing Bubbles — *West Ham United*
- Blue Moon — *Manchester City*
- Marching on Together — *Leeds United*

   *Other football songs usually involve adding new words to a
famous tune or traditional chant. These songs are usually
extremely derogatory and are therefore unpublishable, but
attending any big football match will usually give any fan the
opportunity to hear countless examples of this type of song.*

JOINING THE SUPPORTERS' CLUB

Supporters' clubs have long been a part of the football fan subculture. Traditionally, they played a role in keeping fans informed
about the goings-on at their club by producing newsletters
and fanzines, and also organised tickets and transport to away
matches. Today, most supporters' clubs are affiliated with their
teams, but this has not prevented them from being vocal in their
opposition to unpopular decisions. Supporters' clubs are also
common in countries where there are significant numbers
of expatriates, such as the USA and Australia, and they often
organise screenings of matches.

Pocket Fact 🏆

*The Manchester United Supporters' Trust has been organising a
protest against the current team owners, the Glazer family, by
encouraging fans to wear green and yellow scarves — the colours
of Newton Heath, the original name of Manchester United.*

AWAY GAMES

The most committed fans of a football club have always been
regarded as those who are willing to sacrifice time and effort to

travel to away games. Away supporters are always greatly outnumbered by the home crowd and therefore they tend to be more vocal and passionate in their support for their team, and often develop a sense of community camaraderie. Many smaller teams organise supporters' buses to transport their fans to away games; for larger teams, separate supporters' clubs also take on this responsibility.

Well-travelled fans

Many fans dedicate themselves to following their team – they attend every home game and spend a great deal of time travelling to away games throughout the season. However, there are two sets of fans that deserve special mention in terms of the difficulties they have faced in order to follow their team:

- ***Plymouth Argyle****. During the 2009–2010 season, Plymouth fans faced a long trek to follow their team: Plymouth's closest neighbours in the Championship were Bristol City, who were almost 120 miles away. However, this was a short stroll compared to the away trip to Newcastle United: the round trip to Newcastle and back involved travelling over 800 miles.*

- ***Inverness Caledonian Thistle****. Following Inverness during the 2004–2005 season was a mammoth undertaking. Not only did Inverness fans face long away trips to Glasgow (171 miles), Edinburgh (157 miles) and Kilmarnock (194 miles), they also were forced to travel 104 miles to watch their home games. This was because Inverness' ground did not meet the criteria required by the Scottish Premier League, and so the club were forced to play their home games in Aberdeen for the first half of the season while the stadium was upgraded. Any fan devoted (or insane) enough to travel to all Inverness' league games during the 2004–2005 season would have clocked up over 8,000 miles, the equivalent of travelling from Inverness to Tehran and back.*

FOOTBALL FIRMS

Firms are groups of 'supporters' who are more interested in fighting than football; they have been a constant stain on the history of football, but were especially active during the 1970s and 1980s in the British game. During this period, established gangs, who would stand together at the grounds and wear similar styles of clothing, formed at many clubs. Prominent football firms included the Headhunters (Chelsea), the Suicide Squad (Burnley), and the Bushwhackers (Millwall). Hooliganism began to die out in Britain in the 1990s with the introduction of stricter policing, better organised stewarding and all-seater stadiums.

👟 RADIO, NEWSPAPERS AND 👟 THE INTERNET: FOOTBALL'S COMPLAINTS DEPARTMENT

Football fans excel at one thing above all else: complaining. An entire subculture has grown up to allow football fans to have a good moan about the players they hate, the referees they think are biased and the managers who appear to be saboteurs in the employ of the opposition. Football fans with a lot to get off their chests have many places to turn to:

- **Radio phone-ins**. Football phone-ins are usually to be found on weeknights on local radio stations. These programmes give fans the chance to share their thoughts with the wider community. The shows are often hosted by famous ex-players and the contributors regularly provide one of the greatest sources of unintentional comedy in the modern world. Balanced and coherent opinions are commonly in the extreme minority and no phone-in is complete without at least one call being cut short after the contributor gets a little overheated.

- **Internet message boards**. Internet message boards allow any fan with access to a computer the opportunity to communicate their views to other fans. Message boards can be split into two categories: those that are moderated, such as official club websites or newspaper websites; and those that have no moderation, such as unofficial fan clubs. Moderated boards can often produce some sensible questions and debate, along with insults and taunting of rivals. In contrast, the un-moderated boards are usually filled with wild and unfounded speculation and crude humour.

- **Newspaper letters pages**. Since newspaper editors can choose what to print, the sports letters pages tend to be home to intelligent contributions by fans who have put some serious thought into their opinions, in theory at least. Careful examination of the letters pages will reveal that this is not always the case.

🥾 BITTER RIVALRIES 🥾

For many fans, a successful season is not judged on how many trophies their team wins, or how high they finish in the league; instead it is based on how well their team does in relation to their rivals. A team may have its most successful year, but if they are out-performed by their greatest adversary, then many fans will view the season as a disaster. Often the fiercest rivalries have their origins in the differing social groups that support each team.

- **Boca Juniors and River Plate (Argentina)**. River Plate and Boca Juniors are Argentina's most prominent football teams. Both sides are from Buenos Aires, with Boca's support traditionally based in the working class, while River's fan base has been rooted in the upper classes. The match between the two sides is known as the Superclásico.

- **Rangers and Celtic (Scotland)**. The animosity between Rangers and Celtic is rooted not only in football, but also in religion and politics. Celtic have strong ties to the Catholic community in Glasgow, while Rangers are associated with the Protestant community. This has led to near-constant tension between the two sides since they first met over a century ago. The tension often boils over both during and after matches between the two sides, which are referred to as 'Old Firm derbies'.

- **Fenerbahçe and Galatasaray (Turkey)**. Turkish football fans are known for their passion, but the hostility between Istanbul's two most successful clubs – Fenerbahçe and Galatasaray – is by far the most vitriolic. Fenerbahçe are from the Asian side of the city, while Galatasaray are from the European side, and the matches between the two sides are among the most violent in football, with rioting in the streets common both before and after the matches.

- **Olympiacos and Panathinaikos (Greece)**. Any match between Olympiacos and Panathinaikos is referred to as the 'Derby of the Eternal Enemies'. The two Athens-based teams traditionally attracted fans from different social classes: Panathinaikos' fans were more commonly from the upper classes, while Olympiacos, who are located in the port area of Athens, were followed by the working classes. While this distinction has faded over the years, the animosity between the two sides remains.

- **Al-Ahly and Zamalek (Egypt)**. Both Al-Ahly and Zamalek can claim to be not only the most successful clubs in Egypt, but also in the whole of Africa. Matches between the two Cairo-based clubs excite interest not only in Egypt, but also across the whole of Arabia. Zamalek are traditionally the club of the Egyptian aristocracy, while Al-Ahly are associated with the working classes.

Pocket Fact 🏆

The rivalry between Al-Ahly and Zamalek is so intense that the Egyptian FA decided to bring in foreign referees to oversee matches between the two teams, to prevent accusations of bias.

👟 **FAMOUS FANS** 👟

Sometimes faces in the crowd are more famous than those on the pitch. Some celebrities have followed a team all their life, and some have become supporters for more bizarre reasons. Celebrity football supporters include:

- **Robbie Williams: Port Vale**. Williams was brought up supporting Port Vale and continued to follow them after he became famous. He holds a significant number of Port Vale shares and stipulated that he would only write a song for the FIFA 2000 computer game if Port Vale were included as one of the teams.

- **Cameron Diaz: Brentford**. Diaz became a fan of the London-based League One club after hearing about them from Dan Tana, life-long Brentford fan and owner of a popular Hollywood restaurant.

- **Delia Smith: Norwich**. The world-famous chef is, along with her husband, the major shareholder in the club. Under Smith's stewardship, Norwich managed to gain promotion to the Premier League for the 2004–2005 season. This led to Delia's most famous moment in connection with the club: during half time of a Premier League match against Manchester City, she attempted to rouse the crowd with the words, 'Let's be having you'. It failed to have the desired effect and resulted in much press ridicule.

- **Sean Bean: Sheffield United**. *Lord of the Rings* actor Sean Bean is a well-known Sheffield United fan: he has a tattoo that reads '100% Blade' (a reference to Sheffield United's nickname) and was a director of the club until 2007. Bean also played the role of a Sheffield United player in the film *When Saturday Comes*.

- **Björn Borg: Charlton Athletic**. Swedish tennis legend Borg has been a fan of the south-east London club all his life. His grandfather had first been drawn to the club after they played a series of friendlies in Sweden and passed his love of Charlton to his son, who in turn passed it on to Björn.

- **Alastair Campbell: Burnley**. The former Labour spin doctor grew up not far from Burnley's Turf Moor ground and has been a supporter of the club all his life. He writes an internet blog discussing the ups and downs in the club's fortunes.

- **The Chuckle Brothers: Rotherham United**. The famous children's entertainers, who grew up in Rotherham, played an important role in the 'Save the Millers' campaign when the club was threatened by bankruptcy. They were made honorary life presidents of the team in 2007.

- **Zippy: Dundee United**. Zippy, the loud and often annoying puppet from the children's television programme *Rainbow*, was revealed to have been a Dundee United supporter by Geoffrey Hayes, the presenter of the show. Zippy went on to win a BBC poll of the most popular celebrity football fan, beating the likes of Elton John, Sean Bean and Delia Smith.

- **Elton John: Watford**. Elton John grew up not far from Vicarage Road, Watford's home ground, and grew up as a fan of the team. In 1975, Elton decided to take over the struggling club (they were languishing in the fourth tier of the league) and thanks to his investment, they finished second in the top division in 1983 and reached the FA Cup final in 1984.

Pocket Fact 🏆

It was reported in early 2010 that Sean 'Puff Daddy' Combs was in talks to take control of ailing London club Crystal Palace, but the rapper did not go through with the purchase.

👟 GOING THE EXTRA MILE: 👟
FOOTBALL'S BEST FANS

Every football fan loves their team and by following them, sacrifices time, money and occasionally good health. However, there are some groups of supporters who have gained a reputation for the devotion they have shown to their respective teams. Some are famed for their passion, some for their good humour and others for their eccentricities. Teams whose fans view football not simply as a game, but as a lifestyle choice include:

- **Newcastle United**. Newcastle United's fans are known as the Toon Army (in reference to the Geordie pronunciation of the word 'town') and are famous for the enthusiasm they have for their club. The club has failed to match the success of other English teams, but this has not diminished the passion the supporters have for their club. During the 2009–2010 season, Newcastle boasted the fifth highest average attendance in England, even though they were playing in the Championship.

- **FC St Pauli**. Fans of the Hamburg-based club St Pauli are probably the most progressive supporters in the world. The supporters have a long history of championing socially inclusive policies such as anti-racist and anti-sexist campaigns, and the club was the first in Germany to ban right-wing groups. St Pauli fans also have strong links to the German punk subculture, and many punk artists have been known to wear the St Pauli strip.

- **Scotland National Team**. Followers of the Scottish national team are known as the Tartan Army, and they have become famous throughout Europe and the wider world for their good humour and party atmosphere. The Tartan Army did not always have this reputation; in the 1960s and 1970s, Scottish fans were better known for their violence and drunkenness, but a concerted effort led by football authorities and fans' groups has caused a monumental shift in the behaviour and reception of the Tartan Army abroad. The Tartan Army received awards for their behaviour at both the 1992 European Championships in Sweden and the 1998 World Cup in France.

MONEY WELL SPENT? MONEY AND FOOTBALL

Football is a game before a product, a sport before a market, a show before a business.
Michel Platini

Money has become an increasingly important part of football: talented players can claim astronomical salaries, big clubs can charge huge ticket prices, and television companies can put a large premium on watching the game from the comfort of an armchair. Money talks, and in many cases it has told the game which path to take; however, there has always been an underlying feeling among fans that making money should not be the main aim of football clubs, and this belief continues to this day.

👟 WAGES 👟

THE PAST

Football began as an amateur sport (meaning that players could not be paid), but the teams from the north of England were dominated by working-class men who could not afford to take time off work to play the game unless they were compensated. By 1885, the FA had legalised professionalism and the modern age of paid footballers had begun. However, there were a series of battles between clubs, players, and the football authorities over how much a footballer could be paid. Here are the important milestones in this dispute:

- **1901** The Football League in England imposes a wage cap, limiting the maximum wage for football players to £4 per week.

- **1907** Football players in England form the Association of Football Players' and Trainers' Union to fight for an end to the wage cap, and better rights for players.

- **1920** The weekly wage limit is raised to £9.

- **1947** The weekly wage limit is raised to £12.

- **1956** Jimmy Hill becomes secretary of the Players' Union and changes its name to the Professional Footballers' Association – the name it has continued under to this day.

- **1961** The maximum wage cap is abolished.

Half Time Quiz ⚽

After the wage cap was abolished, who became the first player in Britain to earn £100 per week?
(Answer: The Fulham forward, Johnny Haynes.)

THE PRESENT

In today's game, top football players can expect to earn as much as A-list actors and rock stars. In football's early years when the wage cap was still in place, footballers earned around two or three times the average wage; however, the difference between the two wages has grown exponentially in the last 20 years and today footballers in the English Premier league earn around 30 times the average wage. Footballers also often earn additional money through bonuses, such as goal bonuses and win bonuses, and many are also handsomely paid for endorsing products.

Pocket Fact 🏆

Cristiano Ronaldo was the highest paid footballer in the world during the 2009–2010 season: the Real Madrid star earned over £11 million in this period.

THE FUTURE

The huge growth in football wages has caused concern amongst football officials in both UEFA and FIFA. They view the high levels of spending on wages as unsustainable – a view supported by the plight of Portsmouth, who went into administration towards the end of the 2009–2010 season with debts of over £100 million, partly due to the fact that their wage bill exceeded their annual revenue. UEFA is proposing a limit on club spending, linking the amount any team can spend on wages with the amount of revenue it creates. UEFA also wants to limit the amount of money that wealthy owners can invest in the club, which will prevent what the UEFA president, Michel Platini, calls 'financial doping'. These planned changes have been opposed by many of Europe's top clubs.

Worth every penny? Footballers who have, and have not, earned their pay

Some football players have shown great loyalty and dedication to football by choosing to play for reduced wages to help out a club, whilst others have shown loyalty only to themselves by collecting huge wages and giving nothing in return. Here are some examples of loyalty to football, and loyalty to money:

- *__Mido and West Ham United.__ The Egyptian forward Mido, who had played for Ajax, Tottenham, and Wigan, signed on loan for West Ham United mid-way through the 2009–2010 season. He wanted to prove that he was good enough to play in the English Premier League and because of this, accepted a wage of £1,000 a month, rumoured to be the lowest player's wage in the league.*

- *__Damiano Tommasi and Roma.__ During a friendly match against Stoke City in 2004, Tommasi suffered a knee injury that kept him out of football for over a year. Due to this, he demanded that his contract was re-negotiated so that he was paid the Italian national minimum wage, as he did not want to receive a large salary for sitting on the sidelines.*

He did eventually recover and returned to the Roma first team.

- **Winston Bogarde and Chelsea.** *Dutch international Winston Bogarde's Chelsea contract was worth £40,000 a week over four years. During his four year stay at Chelsea, Bogarde made a grand total of 12 appearances, but Chelsea were unable to sell him because no other team were willing to meet his wage demands. In the end, Bogarde earned around £700,000 per appearance, before leaving the club and retiring from football in 2004.*

👞 BEST AND WORST TRANSFERS 👞

Signing the right players is the key to any team's success. Managers who can spot talent and potential are therefore worth their weight in gold, while managers who cannot are not even worth their weight in half time pies. Football is littered with stories of great signings who have heralded the beginning of a golden age, and terrible signings who have brought a famine of success. Here are the top five best and worst transfers:

BEST TRANSFERS

1. **Eric Cantona (£1.2 million, Leeds United to Manchester United 1992).** During the 1991–1992 season, Leeds United had beaten Manchester United to the League title thanks in part to the talents of Eric Cantona. Alex Ferguson realised that his team lacked a talented forward player and he decided to sign Cantona to fill this hole. Manchester United went on to win the 1992–1993 League title, while Leeds finished 17th. Cantona became Manchester United's key player, helping them to win four League titles in the five years he was with the club.

2. **Henrik Larsson (£650,000, Feyenoord to Celtic 1997).** Henrik Larsson is a legend among Celtic fans: during his time at the club, he helped them win four League titles and

three Scottish Cups, as well as scoring two goals in their 3–2 defeat to Porto in the UEFA Cup final. Larsson went on to further emphasise his ability when he played a key role in Barcelona's 2–1 Champions League final victory over Arsenal in 2006. To put Larsson's £650,000 fee in perspective, in the same year, Leeds United paid £3.25 million for David Hopkin, Tottenham paid £6 million for Les Ferdinand, and Fiorentina paid £8 million for Andrei Kanchelskis.

3. **Roy Keane (£47,000, Cobh Ramblers to Nottingham Forest 1990).** Roy Keane had impressed Nottingham Forest scouts and moved to the club from Irish semi professional side Cobh Ramblers. He went on to become a key player in the Forest side, helping them reach the 1991 FA Cup final and 1992 League Cup final. In 1993, Alex Ferguson paid a British record £3.75 million pounds to take Keane to Old Trafford, meaning that Keane's value had multiplied by almost a hundredfold in his three years at Forest.

4. **Ossie Ardiles and Ricardo Villa (£700,000, Club Atlético Huracán and Racing Club de Avellaneda to Tottenham Hotspur 1978).** During the 1970s, foreign players were rare in English football, and South American players were almost unheard of, and so it was a huge shock when the Tottenham manager, Keith Burkinshaw, returned from Argentina with two new signings: Ardiles and Villa. Ardiles had been a key player in Argentina's 1978 World Cup win and Europe's biggest teams were keen to sign him, but he decided to move to Tottenham, who had only just been promoted back into England's top division. Villa and Ardiles helped Tottenham win two FA Cups in the early 1980s.

5. **Allan Simonsen (£300,000, Barcelona to Charlton 1982).** Allan Simonsen, the 1977 European Footballer of the Year, decided to move on from Barcelona because they had signed Diego Maradona, and Spanish rules limited the number of foreign players a club could field. He was linked with some of the biggest teams in Europe but elected to sign for Charlton, who were playing the second tier of the Football League.

Simonsen only played 16 games because the club struggled to pay his wages, but his stay brought Charlton to the world's attention.

Pocket Fact 🏆

Nicolas Anelka has been transferred seven times in his career, generating transfer fees of almost £90 million. He has played for PSG, Arsenal, Real Madrid, Liverpool, Manchester City, Fenerbahçe, Bolton Wanderers, and Chelsea.

WORST TRANSFERS

1. **Andriy Shevchenko (£30.8 million, AC Milan to Chelsea 2006).** There can be little doubt that Andriy Shevchenko was an unbelievably talented player: he was European Footballer of the Year in 2004, won the Champions League with AC Milan, and is the third highest goal scorer in European competition. However, during his time at Chelsea he showed only glimpses of his past talent – he only managed nine league goals in his two seasons at the club, and struggled to establish himself in the first team. He was loaned back to AC Milan for the 2008–2009 season and moved to Dynamo Kyiv at the start of the 2009–2010 season.

2. **Massimo Taibi (£4.4 million, Venezia to Manchester United, 1999).** Manchester United's long-serving goalkeeper Peter Schmeichel left the club in 1999 and Alex Ferguson signed the Italian goalkeeper Massimo Taibi to replace him. However, Taibi proved to be an expensive flop; after performing well in his debut game against Liverpool he went on to make a series of catastrophic mistakes in the next three games, which resulted in him being dropped from the starting line up and eventually sold back to Italy, having only made four appearances for the club.

3. **Jonathan Woodgate (£13.4 million, Newcastle United to Real Madrid 2004).** Real Madrid have always had trouble

when signing defenders, but without doubt their most impressive mistake involved the transfer of English centre back Jonathan Woodgate. When Woodgate signed for the Spanish giants in August 2004, he was suffering from a particularly bad injury and did not play for over a year. When he finally made his competitive debut in September 2005, he managed to score an own goal and get himself sent off. Woodgate failed to establish himself in the first team and was loaned to Middlesbrough in 2006, with the move becoming permanent in 2007.

4. **Jean-Alain Boumsong (£8 million, Rangers to Newcastle United 2005).** Boumsong had moved to Rangers on a free transfer at the start of the 2004–2005 season and began the season in excellent form, putting in a number of composed performances. Newcastle manager Graeme Souness was greatly impressed and paid £8 million for Boumsong in the 2005 January transfer window. Although he had a reasonably successful first season at Newcastle, his form soon collapsed and his name became synonymous with defensive errors. He was transferred to Juventus in 2006.

5. **Rafael Scheidt (£4.8 million, Gremio to Celtic 1999).** John Barnes endured a torrid time as Celtic manager during the 1999–2000 season, but one of his greatest mistakes was signing the Brazilian defender Rafael Scheidt for just under £5 million. Scheidt made a grand total of three appearances for the club before being sent off on loan and eventually sold by new manager Martin O'Neill.

Record Transfer Fees

Talented football players are in short supply, but the demand for them is extremely high, and this fact has continually driven up transfer fees throughout football's history. Here are some of the most groundbreaking transfers in the history of the game:

- *1905 Alf Common – Sunderland to Middlesbrough: £1,000*
- *1922 Syd Puddefoot – West Ham to Falkirk: £5,000*

- *1932* Bernabé Ferreyra – Club Atlético Tigre to River Plate: £23,000
- *1961* Luis Suárez – Barcelona to Internazionale: £152,000
- *1973* Johan Cruyff – Ajax to Barcelona: £922,000
- *1975* Giuseppe Savoldi – Bologna to Napoli: £1.2 million
- *1984* Diego Maradona – Barcelona to Napoli: £5 million
- *1992* Jean-Pierre Papin – Marseille to AC Milan: £10 million
- *1996* Alan Shearer – Blackburn Rovers to Newcastle United: £15 million
- *1999* Christian Vieri – Lazio to Internazionale: £32 million
- *2001* Zinedine Zidane – Juventus to Real Madrid: £45.6 million
- *2009* Cristiano Ronaldo – Manchester United to Real Madrid: £80 million

FOOTBALL AND ADVERTISING

Corporate sponsorship plays an important role in the modern game, providing clubs and organisations with a stable income source. The main forms of football advertising are:

SHIRT SPONSORSHIP

Shirt sponsorship was pioneered in Britain by Kettering Town in 1976, but the FA forced the club to remove the advertising from their strip after only one outing. The first team to officially wear a sponsored shirt were Liverpool, who played in a sponsored strip from 1979 after the FA ended their ban on football strip advertising. Since that time, shirt sponsorship has grown into a multi-million pound industry, with both Manchester United and Liverpool signing sponsorship deals worth £20 million annually from the beginning of the 2010–2011 season. Aston Villa bucked the trend of selling sponsorship on their strip; they allowed the charity Acorns Children's Hospice to advertise on their strip for free during the 2008–2009 and 2009–2010 seasons.

Pocket Fact 🏆

Barcelona have never allowed corporate advertising on their strips, but since the start of the 2006–2007 season they have worn the UNICEF logo on their shirts, and have made an annual donation to the charity.

STADIUM SPONSORSHIP

Selling the naming rights for a stadium first became popular in the United States, but the idea has spread to Europe in recent years. Arsenal (the Emirates Stadium), Leicester City (the Walkers Stadium), and Bolton (the Reebok Stadium) in the United Kingdom have all opted to take advantage of this revenue stream.

Pocket Fact 🏆

UEFA do not allow stadiums to use their sponsorship names during UEFA competitions, such as the Europa League or the Champions League.

👞 THE FOOTBALL POOLS 👞

The Football Pools was a type of gambling which involved predicting the results of professional football matches that took place in the UK over a week. The original Football Pools company, the Littlewoods Pools, was formed in 1923 by John Moores. The Football Pools gave players the opportunity to win a large amount of money, and the concept of the game was:

- Each player would attempt to select eight matches that would end in a score draw (for example, 1–1 or 2–2).

- If a player picked correctly and all eight selections ended in score draws, then they would win a share of the top prize.

- For a player to win a large amount of money, they had to pick eight score draws in a week that either very few or no other players made a correct selection on.

The first six figure Pools win occurred during the 1950–1951 season, and the first seven figure win happened in the 1985–1986 season. The Pools entered into decline after the introduction of the National Lottery in 1994, but does still continue to this day.

Pocket Fact 🏆

Ironically, the highest ever win on the Football Pools, £2,924,622, happened in the same week that the National Lottery began.

FOOTBALL GAMBLING SCANDALS

Football can be the beautiful game, but there is a side to it that can also be extremely ugly. Football fans invest a lot of time, money, and emotion into following football and in return they expect the game to be honest. However, there have been a few occasions when players and officials have stained the reputation of the game by fixing matches for profit.

Top Football gambling scandals

- **1915.** Seven players were banned from football for life for fixing a match between Liverpool and Manchester United that took place in April 1915. The players had placed bets on the score finishing 2–0 to United. Six of the seven players had their bans lifted because of their service during World War One.

- **1964.** Three Sheffield Wednesday players – David Layne, Peter Swan, and Tony Kay, along with the ex-player Jimmy Gauld – conspired to fix a 1962 Sheffield Wednesday match against Ipswich Town. Gauld revealed the fix to a Sunday newspaper in 1964, and the four players were given jail sentences and banned from football for life.

- **1980.** AC Milan and Lazio were both demoted to Serie B in Italy after an investigation revealed widespread match-fixing in Italy's top two divisions, in what became known as the Totonero Scandal. The Italian striker Paolo Rossi was implicated in the scandal and was initially banned from football for three years, but this was reduced to two years on appeal. This reduction allowed Rossi to participate in the 1982 World Cup: a tournament that Italy would win with Rossi finishing as top scorer.

- **2005.** German referees Robert Hoyzer and Dominik Marks were sent to prison and banned from football for life after admitting to betting on matches that they had refereed. Three Croatian brothers were also implicated in the match-fixing scheme and were given prison sentences.

- **2009**: Investigations in Germany revealed a Europe-wide match-fixing conspiracy that was spread across nine countries and involved as many as 200 matches. Nine players from second division Swiss clubs were handed bans in May 2010 as a result of information provided by German police. UEFA promised to make the eradication of match-fixing in football their top priority as a result of the revelations.

Pocket Fact ♛

In 2006, a huge match-rigging scandal involving several Italian clubs was uncovered by Italian police, although the scandal was unconnected to gambling. AC Milan, Juventus, Lazio, Fiorentina, and Reggina had conspired to make sure that their matches were refereed by officials of their choosing. As a consequence of their actions, Juventus were relegated to Serie B and stripped of their last two Serie A titles, while the other four clubs were given points deductions for the following season.

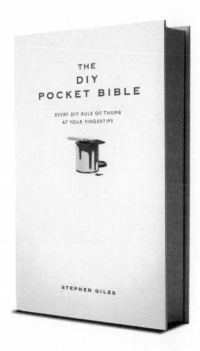

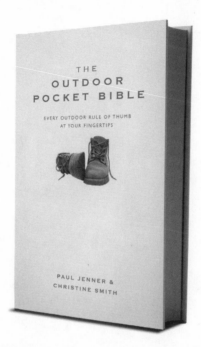

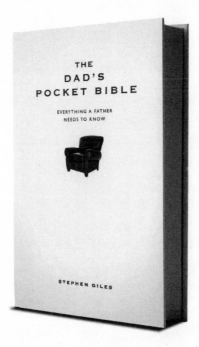

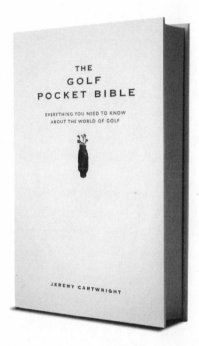

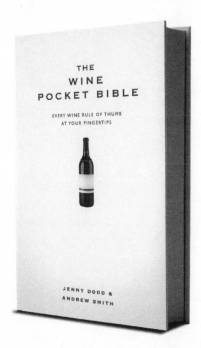